THE EAT YOUR WAY HEALTHY AT TRADER JOE'S COOKBOOK

Over 75 Easy, Delicious Recipes for Every Meal

written and photographed by

Bonnie Matthews

Skyhorse Publishing

The author of this book is not a medical professional. While every effort has been made to provide information on brands and ingredients that are listed as gluten-free, it is the responsibility of the reader or anyone who may use this information to confirm whether they are allergen-free or gluten-free without cross contamination. The author and publisher assume no liability for inaccuracies or misstatements about products or opinions in this book. Some photographs show more than one portion for visual reference. Portion size will vary based on a person's needs.

Skyhorse Publishing books may be purchased in bulk at special discounts for sales promotion, corporate gifts, fund-raising, or educational purposes. Special editions can also be created to specifications. For details, contact the Special Sales Department, Skyhorse Publishing, 307 West 36th Street, 11th Floor, New York, NY 10018 or info@skyhorsepublishing.com.

Skyhorse® and Skyhorse Publishing® are registered trademarks of Skyhorse Publishing, Inc.®, a Delaware corporation.

Visit our website at www.skyhorsepublishing.com.

10 9 8

Library of Congress Cataloging-in-Publication Data is available on file.

Cover design by Georgia Morrissey
Cover photo by Bonnie Matthews

ISBN: 978-1-63450-652-6
Ebook ISBN: 978-1-63450-653-3

Printed in China

In memory of Jennifer Johnson, a.k.a. JJ,
my dear friend and old housemate whom I met at Trader Joe's.
Special thanks to my foodie friends, Arabella Girardi and Alysia Gadson,
for helping me with the book.

Table of Contents

Chapter 6 — Prep for Success ... 155

Chapter 7 — Date Night ... 187

Introduction

How is it possible to love a grocery store? I mean, it's only four walls, freezer cases, and shelves full of food, right? Wrong. My friend, Karen, introduced me to Trader Joe's when I visited her in Tucson, Arizona. She was adamant about me going to Trader Joe's while I was there. I had no idea why she was making such a big deal over a grocery store, but once I stepped inside I was fascinated. It had personality. There was a colorful, welcoming sign and pleasant employees. Inside it smelled like fresh flowers, and the merchandise and products were unique and inexpensive.

I admired the store's dedication to healthy foods, which included an entire aisle of dried fruits and nuts. The brand was also creative with salsas, combining spices and fruits in ways I never would have imagined. With delicious coffees made with beans from all over the world for just a few bucks, I was hooked.

Years later, I was excited when my city, Baltimore, got its first Trader Joe's. This little store helped save my life, literally. Around 2008 I was going through a seriously difficult time in my life. I was a freelance illustrator and my career took a big blow due to the economy's downward spiral. My seven year relationship had just ended and I didn't know how I was going to pay the mortgage. I was so depressed.

Then it hit me. I love to cook, and my local Trader Joe's was looking for a part-time demo person. Dennis, the store's Captain, asked me, "What is your favorite product in the store?" When I told him it was the White Stilton Cheese with Mango and Ginger, he hired me on the spot.

Honestly, I needed the job for more than just the measly hourly wage, I needed the medical benefits. They offer full medical benefits for part-time employees. That job was gold to me, and it helped me to start living a healthier lifestyle.

I had gotten up to nearly 300 pounds around that time, and I needed a change. Believe it or not, being surrounded by food all day at work enabled me to really focus on my body.

I was on a mission to drop 130 pounds, and I found my secret weapon at Trader Joe's! I met two customers: Kenny and his wife. They came in all the time wearing workout clothes, and they bought healthy food. He noticed I had been losing weight and asked how I was doing it. I told him I was cutting out ice cream and cheese, and I had started walking for exercise. Then he told me he was a personal trainer and could help me. "I don't have money for a trainer," I said.

"I'll make you a deal, if you come see me for a month and you don't see any results in pounds or inches lost, I'll give you all your money back."

I tried it, and after some crying, kicking, and screaming, I lost eight pounds and dropped two inches in my waistline that month. I was hooked!

I had always loved to cook. My dad was a stay-at-home parent and cooked for our family. He made the best fried chicken ever and was an incredible baker. His specialties were breads, pies, and cakes. I grew up eating the wrong foods, but food had to become my friend and not my enemy. Creativity with food was going to be a part of my newfound healthy lifestyle. I also had a ten percent discount to buy food at Trader Joe's. I had to make peace with food and make better choices or I knew that I would not be able to survive.

After two years of dedication, focus, and a lot of hard work, I did drop about 130 pounds. People would ask, "How could you possibly drop all that weight while being surrounded by food all day?" I'd respond, "You gotta want it more than pizza."

After appearing on *The Dr. Oz Show* to discuss my weight loss transformation and healthy recipes, I became well-known for my cooking. After my nine minutes of fame in front of 17 million viewers, Dr. Oz dubbed me a "Wellness Warrior." He offered me a blog on DoctorOz.com to celebrate and share with people my views on life, food, and fitness. And so began my career as a cookbook author and motivator for healthy lifestyle choices. *The Eat Your Way Healthy at Trader Joe's Cookbook* is my fourth book.

I never would have imagined in a million years that I would love fitness, writing, and eating healthy foods. I hope this book inspires you to explore new flavors and foods, and motivates you toward a healthier lifestyle. It's never too late to reinvent yourself.

I hope you enjoy the meals and beverages I've put together and can enjoy these recipes with your family and friends at home. Meanwhile, I'm going to keep stirring, chopping, and smiling.

With gratitude,
Bonnie

About the Book

There is a little bit of everything in this book. Some recipes are easy meal ideas, while others are more creative recipes. I've come up with these recipes using fresh produce and meats as well as special spices and sauces exclusively available at Trader Joe's—like the Green Dragon Sauce.

The title "Eat Your Way Healthy" refers to just that. Not everyone likes the same foods. Not everyone even prepares a recipe the same way twice. So use these recipe ideas and add to them. Experiment! Make substitutions. Be inspired by new flavors and vegetables! Have fun seeing what you and your family enjoy and see what meal combinations work best for you and your health goals.

Many of the recipes can make servings of four or six, so if you are a single person or a couple, portion out the meals into sealed containers to take to work or eat as leftovers. If you're super ambitious you may want to make a recipe or two on Sunday and portion them out so you can have quick meals ready to heat and eat. It's little tricks like these that truly help keep portion sizes to a minimum and avoid high calorie take-out food.

The recipes here are not necessarily part of a specific diet plan, but rather a way to start thinking about being more mindful with eating, and that starts with preparing your meals. It's best to eat clean, meaning less processed, less refined products that contain very little or no additives or chemicals.

Though Trader Joe's is not specifically a healthy food store, they have done a great job offering a really great selection of organic products and all natural products that contain very little or no additives or preservatives. They offer hormone-free milks, cheeses, and meats. Kudos to TJ's for offering them also at very low prices.

Do yourself a favor, get yourself a good sharp knife for all those veggies you're going to be chopping. Buy a stack of good clear food containers for leftovers and portioned out meals. Get rid of the processed foods in your fridge. Clean out the freezer. Give all the cookies and enriched flour breads and pastas to a neighbor, and get ready to start fresh!

Set yourself up for successful health goals and enjoy delicious meals!

chapter 1

Wake Up! Shape Up!

Recipes and simple meal ideas that are packed with protein to rev up your body before or after your workout.

Makes 1-2 servings

Get yourself a mini, single-serve skillet and have some fun using all sorts of leftover veggies! I used kabocha squash and Murasaki sweet potatoes for this recipe. Both offer a great nutty sweetness with the benefits of complex carbs and fiber. Well, alrighty then!

BREAKFAST FRITTATA

canola cooking spray or coconut oil spray

2 eggs, whisked with Himalayan pink salt and pepper

1 link All Natural Sweet Apple Chicken Sausage, browned, diced

½–¾ cup kabocha squash, peeled, diced, and roasted

½–¾ cup Murasaki sweet potato, diced and roasted

1 cup fresh baby spinach, loosely chopped

4–5 heirloom grape tomatoes

2 tablespoons crumbled goat cheese

fresh cracked pepper

½ avocado, chopped

Coat skillet with cooking spray and place on stove over medium heat. Toss in all ingredients except the avocado and cover. Cook for approximately 5–8 minutes, until the eggs are firm and fully cooked. Top with the avocado and serve with a mild salsa if desired.

Roasting Kabocha Squash

Preheat oven to 400°F.

With a large chef's knife, carefully pierce the skin of the squash and cut it into quarters. Then, cut each quarter in half to make 3-inch pieces. Remove the seeds and fibers with a spoon and discard. Spray with canola oil or drizzle a little olive oil on the flesh side of the squash. Place on a baking sheet lined with parchment paper and bake for 20 minutes or until tender.

Remove from the oven and allow to cool enough so you can handle the pieces. Peel off the skin with a knife, and then cut into ½-inch pieces.

Optional serving suggestion: Serve with a mild salsa.

Note: See page 208 for the Roasting Murasaki Sweet Potatoes recipe and for cooking the All Natural Chicken Apple Sausage.

Makes 1-2 servings

This recipe makes for a delicious and creative breakfast. The Hot Smoked Sockeye Salmon is found in the refrigerator case at Trader Joe's, and it can be used in many ways. You can crumble it onto salads or toss it into egg cups, as seen on page 30. If you haven't had a hot smoked salmon, you're in for a treat! It's got a completely different texture than salmon lox.

HOT SMOKED SALMON
Salad with Farro

½ cup TJ's 10 Minute Farro

1 cup Hot Smoked Sockeye Salmon, crumbled into chunks

2 cups organic baby spinach

½ avocado, diced

1 teaspoon capers

½ cup organic heirloom grape tomatoes, sliced

2 tablespoons red onion, sliced thin

Himalayan pink salt

fresh cracked pepper

Cook 10 Minute Farro according to package instructions, then set aside to cool. Combine remaining ingredients together, adding the farro once it has cooled. Add dressing and serve immediately.

½ cup white balsamic vinegar

3 tablespoons TJ's Sicilian Extra Virgin Olive Oil

2 garlic cloves, smashed and minced

1 teaspoon TJ's Hot & Sweet Mustard

White Balsamic Vinaigrette

Makes enough for 2 salads

Whisk all ingredients together in a bowl, then add to salad and toss.

Note: For a more peppery, garlicky kick, make the dressing an hour ahead of time. It will really flavor up!

Makes 1 serving

This is my go-to pre- or post-workout meal on days when I lift weights.

CHOCOLATE PROTEIN
Smoothie

1 scoop chocolate Designer Whey Protein Powder

1 cup organic, fat-free milk

⅓ frozen banana (previously chopped into bite-size pieces for blending)

1 teaspoon organic virgin coconut oil (liquefied at room temperature)

1 teaspoon Organic Peanut Butter, creamy, salted

Blend all ingredients together in an electric blender, pour into a glass and enjoy.

Options: If desired, blend in ice. You can substitute unsweetened almond milk for the fat-free milk. Choose the one found in the grocery aisle, as the one in the refrigerated case contains sugar.

Makes 1 serving

There's an unlimited amount of variations for this recipe you can come up with using vegetables and the different flavors of sausages found in the refrigerator aisle.

If you can't find a cute little skillet like the one in the photo, make this in a regular skillet as a scramble. The little skillet is adorable, and it's a great way to maintain portion control!

SINGLE EGG SKILLET

1 link TJ's All Natural Sweet
   Apple Chicken Sausage, diced
   and browned
canola spray or clarified butter
2-3 pieces of broccolini,
   roasted ahead of time
1 large organic egg
Himalayan pink salt
fresh cracked pepper

Cook sausage in a skillet over medium heat for approximately 5 minutes, until browned.

Lightly spray mini skillet with cooking spray. Heat on medium. Place broccolini and sausage around the edges of the skillet and break an egg into the center. Lightly cover the skillet and cook egg to your desired firmness.

Add salt and pepper to taste.

2-3 pieces broccolini
olive oil
TJ's Everyday Seasoning

Roasted Broccolini

Preheat oven to 400°F.

Place broccolini in a bowl with a drizzle of olive oil. Sprinkle with the Everyday Seasoning. Transfer to a 9 x 12 casserole dish or baking sheet lined with parchment paper. Roast approximately 13–15 minutes, until the edges start to brown.

Options: There are many variations for this recipe using various vegetables and the different flavors of sausages found in the refrigerator aisle.

The perfect breakfast for a drizzly, cold Sunday when you really don't feel like getting out of bed. Pair this with a pot of Trader Joe's Organic Five Country Espresso Blend, and you're golden!

HOT SMOKED SALMON
Breakfast

2 hard-cooked eggs, peeled

2-3 slices TJ's Hot Smoked Sockeye Salmon (found in the refrigerated case)

6 Marinated Mushrooms with Garlic

2 tablespoons capers

2-3 pieces TJ's European Style Whole Grain Bread

several thin slices of red onion

Dice eggs. Arrange all ingredients on a nice platter or cutting board and serve with a "Good morning" kiss.

½ cup plain nonfat Greek-style yogurt

2 teaspoons organic mayonnaise

3 teaspoons TJ's Whole Grain Dijon Mustard

black pepper to taste

1 teaspoon horseradish

Dijon Aioli

Combine all ingredients in a small bowl and use as a topping for the salmon. Leftover aioli can be stored in the refrigerator for one week.

Makes 12 servings

These little egg cups are a fantastic, portable, high-protein breakfast that can be made ahead of time. I also love them with salad for a light lunch after a workout. You can use any kind of hot smoked salmon, or use leftover grilled salmon from last night's dinner. I used Trader Joe's Wild Smoked Sockeye Salmon.

EGG CUPS with Hot Smoked Salmon

12 eggs

¼ cup fresh basil, diced

½ cup crumbled goat cheese

1-2 cups fresh spinach or baby kale, diced

a few dashes of garlic powder

¼ teaspoon fresh black pepper

Himalayan pink salt or sea salt

cooking spray

8-10 whole wheat tortilla wraps (or any kind you prefer)

1 cup of TJ's Wild Smoked Sockeye Salmon, crumbled into chunks

Preheat oven to 375°F.

In a large bowl, whisk the eggs. Add the basil, goat cheese, spinach or kale, garlic, pepper and salt.

Spray muffin tin with cooking spray. Rip the tortilla wraps into thirds. Line the muffin tin with the wraps, making sure the bottom of each muffin hole is covered with tortilla. The tortilla wraps can extend beyond the height of the pan. Fill each muffin hole almost to the top, leaving room for the salmon. Top each muffin with pieces of salmon. Bake 15–20 minutes, until a toothpick inserted near the center comes out clean and dry.

Option: Add variety to this recipe by including sautéed mushrooms, sweet bell peppers, or diced kale.

Makes 1 serving

This recipe was inspired by my buddy, Joel Harper, celebrity fitness trainer and creator of the Fit Pack DVD series. His original recipe calls for flaxseed milk, but I substituted almond milk. This recipe has natural sweeteners, making it the perfect sweet little afternoon snack. Plus, it's loaded with nutrient-dense ingredients, like hemp seed hearts, that have omega-3 and omega-6 fatty acids, as well as soluble and insoluble fiber. The raw dates offer lean protein and more fiber.

DATE and ALMOND Smoothie

1½ cups unsweetened almond milk

5 raw almonds

3 dates (seeded)

2 tablespoons cocoa powder

4 ice cubes

2 teaspoons hemp seed hearts

½ teaspoon TJ's Stevia Extract

⅓ banana

Combine all ingredients in a NutriBullet or comparable smoothie blender. Pour into a glass for an afternoon snack or post-workout recovery.

Makes 1 serving

Kim Lyons, celebrity trainer and owner of Bionic Body Gym in Hermosa Beach, California, shared this recipe, which I've slightly altered. When Kim interviewed me about my weight loss for her article in *Muscle and Body Magazine* a few years ago, we discovered that we share the same philosophy about muscle training, fitness, and food.

PUMPKIN SPICE SHAKE

¼ cup organic pumpkin (may be seasonal)

½ cup vanilla flavored Coconut Milk or Almond Beverage

¼ tablespoon TJ's Pumpkin Pie Spice

⅓ of a banana

Combine all ingredients in a small blender. Pour into a glass. Add ice to enjoy cold, or heat it up for a warm treat.

Optional: Add one scoop of vanilla Designer Whey Protein Powder if you drink this after a workout. For a sweeter smoothie, add 1 teaspoon of pure maple syrup or ½ teaspoon Trader Joe's Stevia Extract.

Makes 3-4 tomatoes

Heirloom tomatoes are highly irregular in shape and are often referred to as "ugly tomatoes," but don't be fooled by their appearance. They have a rich, robust flavor compared to the bland Hot House varieties that have been hybridized to be perfectly round.

STUFFED HEIRLOOM TOMATOES
with Garlic Chicken Sausage

3-4 large heirloom tomatoes

2 links TJ's All Natural Garlic Herb Chicken Sausage, diced and browned

3 organic eggs

1 cup fresh baby spinach, roughly chopped

3 tablespoons (or more) crumbled goat cheese

Himalayan pink salt to taste

TJ's Everyday Seasoning

Preheat oven to 350°F.

Cut off the top ¼ inch or so of the tomatoes and discard tops. Scoop out the center with a spoon and discard. Spray a 9 × 12 baking dish with cooking spray or line with parchment paper and add tomatoes.

Combine sausage, eggs, spinach, cheese, salt, and seasoning in a bowl.

Portion mixture into each tomato and cover with tinfoil. Bake approximately 30 minutes, or until the egg is visibly opaque and firm.

Eat immediately.

Optional: Top tomatoes with bread crumbs.

---

2 pieces European Style Whole Grain Bread or Ezekiel Bread

2 teaspoons TJ's Everyday Seasoning

1 teaspoon olive oil

Bread Crumb Topping

Preheat oven to 400°F.

Place bread on a baking sheet and bake several minutes until it's dried out. Remove bread from oven and blend it in a food processor or crumble it with a rolling pin. Place crumbs in a bowl with seasoning and olive oil and mix together. Top tomatoes with it about halfway through the cooking time. You can also mix some into the tomato stuffing mixture if desired.

Makes 1 serving

The perfect snack in only 3 minutes!
Sweet potatoes are a good complex carb.
They're packed with vitamins and minerals, as well as fiber, which keep
you feeling satisfied. One medium sweet
potato is only about 103 calories.
Trader Joe's carries organic sweet
potatoes and Murasaki sweet potatoes,
which have a purple skin and white
flesh. They are super sweet!

SWEET POTATO "SPAGHETTI" with Smoked Paprika

1 medium organic sweet potato or
  Murasaki sweet potato with the
  skin on, scrubbed
1 teaspoon clarified butter or
  coconut oil spray
a few shakes of smoked paprika
Himalayan pink salt

Place the potato in the large pasta side of the Veggetti. Carefully turn the potato according to the instructions to create spaghetti-like strands.

Place the "spaghetti" on a microwavable plate. Add the clarified butter or coconut oil, smoked paprika, and salt. Cover with a moistened paper towel and cook for 3 minutes until tender.

Eat immediately.

Note: For this recipe you'll need a Veggetti Spiral Veg-etable Slicer. It can make spaghetti out of any kind of vegetable. It costs around $12 and can be found online or at major department stores.

chapter 2

Green with Envy

Yummy ways to get more greens and veggies into your meals.

According to WholeGrainCouncil.org, consuming sprouted grains, including rice, can help increase HDL-cholesterol (the good cholesterol) levels which aid in lowering the risk of cardiovascular disease. Not only is the Sprouted Rice Medley at Trader Joe's delicious, it is healthy!

SPROUTED RICE "RISOTTO" with Asparagus

1 tablespoon olive oil

½ red onion, diced

1 package TJ's Mushroom Medley (freezer case), thawed

1¼ cup TJ's Sprouted Organic California Rice

2 cups organic chicken broth

1 teaspoon dried thyme

1 cup water

⅓ cup cooking sherry

½ cup grated Parmesan cheese

1 heaping teaspoon goat cheese, any kind

½ package TJ's Grilled Asparagus Spears, thawed and cut into 2-inch lengths

a dash of Himalayan pink salt

fresh parsley, diced

In a large skillet, add olive oil and onion. Cook over medium heat until the onions are translucent and tender. Add mushrooms, rice, chicken broth, thyme, water, and sherry. Cover, reduce heat, and simmer approximately 25 minutes, stirring occasionally. Most liquid should be evaporated or absorbed by the rice, and the rice should be tender. If not, add a few tablespoons of water and continue cooking until rice is tender.

Remove from heat and gently stir in cheeses and asparagus, then season with pink salt as desired. Toss in diced parsley for garnish. Serve immediately.

Makes 3-4 servings

The Keta salmon is pale in color when compared to other salmon varieties, yet it offers a delicious, mild flavor. I suggest using Trader Joe's Extra Virgin California Estate Olive Oil in this recipe. It's made with Arbequina olives, which offer a nice buttery, fruity flavor. Fish can be served on the salad warm or cold.

SALMON SALAD
with Corn and Chili Salsa
with Lime Cumin Vinaigrette

1 package Keta salmon, thawed

TJ's Extra Virgin California Estate Olive Oil

Himalayan pink salt

fresh cracked pepper

1 package TJ's Healthy 8 Chopped Veggie Mix

¾ cup TJ's Corn & Chile Tomato-less Salsa

Preheat oven to 400°F.

Thaw salmon according to package instructions, or defrost in cold water while in packaging for 20 minutes or until thawed. Remove fish from packaging and place in a bowl with olive oil. Lightly salt and pepper. Put the salmon on a baking sheet then place it on the center rack in the oven. Bake approximately 14 minutes, turning once, or until salmon is firm and opaque all the way through.

Place salmon onto the Healthy 8 Chopped Veggie Mix dressed with Lime Cumin Vinaigrette (see page 209) and top with the salsa. Serve family style or portion out onto plates.

In Italian, the word "Arrabiata" means "angry." The Trader Joe's sauce is perfectly named, as it's spiced with red chilies, tomatoes, and garlic.

SPAGHETTI SQUASH with Sausage and Arrabiata Sauce

1 spaghetti squash

cooking spray

Himalayan pink salt

2 links TJ's All Natural Sweet Basil Pesto Smoked Chicken and Turkey Sausage, diced

½ jar of TJ's Arrabiata Sauce

olive oil

fresh basil

Shaved Grana Padano Parmesan

fresh cracked black pepper

Preheat oven to 425°F.

Carefully pierce the skin of the squash with a sharp knife and cut in half lengthwise. Scoop out the seeds and discard. Spray the squash flesh with cooking spray and season with salt. Place squash, flesh side down, in a parchment paper-lined 9 × 12 baking dish. Bake approximately 50 minutes, or until squash is tender when pierced with a fork.

While the squash is cooking, brown the sausage in a skillet over medium heat. Pour the sauce into the skillet and heat through.

When the squash is tender, remove from the oven. Turn it over and fluff the flesh carefully with a fork. It will flake off from the skin and should be easy to remove. Place directly on plate and drizzle with a little olive oil. Top with sausage and sauce. Add basil, cheese, and fresh cracked pepper. Serve immediately.

Note: The arrabiata sauce is wonderfully spicy. If your child is not that adventurous, try one of the other pasta sauces.

Makes 4-5 servings

Farro is a wonderful heirloom grain that's a good source of lean protein and iron. It has a nice nutty flavor and slightly chewy texture. The Trader Joe's brand comes parboiled, so it only takes about 10 minutes to cook.

FARRO SALAD

1 package TJ's 10 Minute Farro

6 ounces (½ container) Trader Joe's Marinated Fresh Mozzarella balls

¼ cup TJ's Julienne Sliced Sun Dried Tomatoes packed in olive oil

½ cup pitted Kalamata olives, chopped

2-3 teaspoons lemon juice

6-8 basil leaves, loosely chopped

1 teaspoon garlic, smashed and minced

a little olive oil from the mozzarella container

fresh cracked pepper

Cook farro according to package instructions, using water or vegetable broth (I prefer using the broth). Allow to cool. While it cools, combine the mozzarella, tomatoes, olives, lemon juice, basil, garlic, olive oil, and pepper in a large bowl. Once farro is cool, add it to the bowl and toss. Taste and add extra lemon or even lemon zest for bright flavor, if desired.

Optional: Add 3 tablespoons of toasted pine nuts for a nutty layer of flavor. Want more protein in this salad? Add some of Trader Joe's Just Chicken, which is fully cooked in the refrigerated section and ready to use in any recipe.

FARRO HASH with
Roasted Brussels Sprouts

2 cups fresh Brussels sprouts, chopped, or use 1 bag of TJ's Shaved Brussels Sprouts

2 teaspoons roasted pistachio oil

Himalayan pink salt

black pepper

2 teaspoons TJ's Balsamic Glaze

1½ cups kabocha squash, roasted and diced

1½ cups Murasaki sweet potatoes, roasted and diced

½ package TJ's 10 Minute Farro

1 tablespoon pure maple syrup

2 dashes dried French thyme (less than ¼ teaspoon)

3 tablespoons raw pumpkin seeds

4 tablespoons crumbled goat cheese

Preheat oven to 400°F.

Drizzle Brussels sprouts with the pistachio oil, then add a little salt and pepper. Place onto a baking sheet lined with parchment paper and bake 20–30 minutes or until tender. (The shaved Brussels sprouts may cook faster.) Remove from oven and place in a bowl. Drizzle with balsamic glaze and set aside.

Cook squash and sweet potatoes in the oven until tender. See the Breakfast Frittata recipe on page 18 for cooking instructions.

Cook farro according to package instructions.

Place Brussels sprouts, squash, sweet potatoes and farro in a bowl and toss together with maple syrup, thyme, and pumpkin seeds. Add the goat cheese and gently toss together. Serve at room temperature or slightly warm.

Makes 3 servings

This spaghetti is a fun way to enjoy decadent flavors without traditional pasta carbs.

GRILLED SPAGHETTI SQUASH

1 large spaghetti squash

½ red onion

2 tablespoons butter or Earth
   Balance Buttery Spread

Parmesan cheese, shaved,
   to taste

sea salt

fresh cracked black pepper

6-7 fresh sage leaves

Grilling the Squash

Preheat gas grill on high with lid closed. If using a charcoal grill, prepare for direct heat cooking over hot charcoal. When using a gas grill, reduce the temperature of the grill to medium–high. Carefully coat the grill surface with cooking spray, spraying at an angle. Don't have a grill? Have no fear, you can prepare the squash in an oven. For oven-cooking instructions, see the recipe for Spaghetti Squash with Chicken and Arrabiata Sauce on page 46.

Cut the squash lengthwise and remove the pulp and seeds. Coat with olive oil or cooking spray and place on a large piece of heavy-duty aluminum foil, folding up the edges to seal the squash completely. Place directly on the grill grate and cook for 10 minutes, then turn over and cook another 6–8 minutes, until the squash is tender all the way through. Remove the squash from the grill, but keep it wrapped in the aluminum foil while preparing the sauce.

While the squash is cooking, slice the onion into ½-inch-thick discs. Coat with a little cooking oil and place directly on grill grate for 2–3 minutes per side, until tender. Remove onion from the grill and transfer to a cutting board to cool. Dice and set aside.

Remove the aluminum foil and fluff the squash with a fork. Add a tablespoon of butter to each half. Add in Parmesan, salt and pepper to taste, diced sage leaves, and the onions. Sprinkle the top with a few more shavings of Parmesan and garnish with sage leaves. Serve immediately.

Makes 4-6 servings

Is it fall, or is it that I just love kabocha squash all the time? For a variation on this recipe, use the fresh butternut squash from the produce department. It's already cut up and ready to roast, making it very convenient.

CURRIED BARLEY
and Kabocha Squash

2 cups kabocha squash, cubed and roasted

1 package TJ's 10 Minute Barley

1 teaspoon clarified butter or olive oil

½ fresh red bell pepper, diced

2 teaspoons onion (optional)

3 cloves garlic, smashed and minced

3 teaspoons curry powder

½ cup raw pumpkin seeds

½ cup dried cranberries

1 can organic garbanzo beans, rinsed and drained

a dash of cayenne pepper

Himalayan pink salt

black pepper

See the Breakfast Frittata recipe on page 18 for instructions on roasting kabocha squash.

Cook barley according to package instructions.

Heat butter or olive oil in a sauce pan over medium heat. Add red bell pepper, onion, garlic, and curry powder. Cook vegetables 4–5 minutes or until tender. Transfer to a large bowl and mix together with squash, barley, and remaining ingredients. Taste and adjust seasoning as desired. I personally like a little more curry.

Optional: Add sweetness and texture with diced dried apricot.

Makes 2 hearty servings

This is my go-to salad when I want to trim a few inches from my waistline. I presented this recipe on *The Dr. Oz Show*, as it was one of the recipes that helped in my 120-pound weight loss. Sardines are a part of my healthy snack options. They are loaded with protein, good fatty acids, and have zero carbs. If you don't think you'll enjoy sardines, substitute canned yellowfin tuna or canned smoked trout.

SARDINE SALAD with Balsamic Dressing

1 bag baby mixed greens

1 can TJ's Lightly Smoked Sardines in Olive Oil

small handful of cranberries (or diced fresh pear when in season)

3 tablespoons raw or roasted pumpkin seeds

3 tablespoons crumbled goat cheese

Toss together the greens, sardines, cranberries, pumpkin seeds, and goat cheese. Set aside.

¼ cup TJ's Balsamic Vinegar of Modena (the small square jar with the red label, not the one in the jug)

¼ cup honey

3 tablespoons TJ's Hot & Sweet Mustard

3-4 cloves fresh garlic, smashed and minced

Bonnie's Balsamic Dressing

Whisk together the vinegar, honey, mustard, and garlic. Test and adjust to taste.

Dress the salad and serve.

Note: I don't use olive oil in this recipe, but you can add some if you like.

Makes 6 servings

Trader Joe's has fresh, raw beets as well as fully cooked, vacuum-packed beets in their refrigerator case. Beets taste good hot or cold, and they're also a great source of antioxidants. These low-calorie purple beauties are packed with nutrients. I love them raw, shaved into a salad, or cooked.

BEET AND BARLEY SALAD

1 package TJ's 10 Minute Barley

1 package TJ's Steamed & Peeled Baby Beets

4-6 tablespoons roasted, salted pistachios

3-4 tablespoons crumbled goat cheese

2-3 teaspoons apple cider vinegar

Himalayan pink salt

fresh cracked pepper

fresh mint, chopped

roasted pistachio oil or olive oil

Cook barley according to package instructions. (The barley will taste better if you use vegetable broth!) Allow to cool.

While the barley cools, combine the beets, pistachios, goat cheese, vinegar, salt, pepper, mint, and a drizzle of oil in a large bowl. Add the cooled barley and gently stir. Serve chilled.

Option: This salad is also delicious with white beans or garbanzo beans.

Makes 2 servings

I grew up in Virginia, where coleslaw was made with a lot of mayonnaise, vinegar, and sugar. I've dialed back the mayo and added more vegetables for a healthier version of my dad's old recipe. The Cruciferous Crunch Collection is loaded with kale, Brussels sprouts, and green and red cabbage. Plus, it's ready to use, no chopping necessary!

CRUCIFEROUS SLAW

1 tablespoon apple cider vinegar

1 tablespoon honey

⅓ cup plain nonfat Greek-style yogurt

2 tablespoons organic mayonnaise

½ package TJ's Cruciferous Crunch Collection

Combine vinegar, honey, yogurt, and mayonnaise in a large bowl. Toss in Cruciferous Crunch Collection and serve.

Options: You can add 5 ounces of shredded carrots. If you do, add a little more vinegar and 2 tablespoons of yogurt.

To spice up your coleslaw, add 2 teaspoons of whole grain Dijon mustard and ½ teaspoon horseradish.

Makes about 2 servings

A perfect salad that pairs well with most any baked fish. For this recipe you'll need to use a Veggetti Spiral Vegetable Slicer or similar tool. You can use the premade Asian Style Spicy Peanut Vinaigrette (located in the refrigerator case) as is, or dress it up a little to make it even more flavorful.

SPICY ASIAN RAINBOW Carrots

3-4 TJ's Organic Carrots of Many Colors, shaved into "spaghetti"

¼ cup TJ's Asian Style Spicy Peanut Vinaigrette

a dash of cayenne pepper

2 teaspoons rice vinegar

1 teaspoon toasted sesame seed oil (optional)

1 tablespoon smooth peanut butter

fresh diced cilantro

Using the slicer, shave the carrots into "spaghetti."

Combine the vinaigrette, pepper, vinegar, oil, and peanut butter in a small bowl. Toss in the carrots and stir. Garnish with the cilantro and serve.

Optional: For a spicier, crunchier salad, add chopped TJ's Thai Lime and Chili Cashews!

Note: Don't have a vegetable slicer? No worries, you can make this salad with grated carrots instead.

Makes 4-5 servings

Did you get invited to a party at the last minute? Here's a recipe for a great salad you can make in a jiffy using the fully cooked brown rice from Trader Joe's that only takes 3 minutes to reheat.

SERRANO SALSA SALAD

1 pouch TJ's Organic Brown Rice (freezer case)

1 container TJ's Serrano Salsa Fresca (refrigerated section)

1 avocado, diced

½ medium red onion

1 can organic black beans, rinsed and drained

1 cup TJ's Roasted Corn (freezer case), thawed

½ bunch fresh cilantro, diced

1-2 limes, juiced

a pinch of Himalayan pink salt

Heat brown rice according to instructions, then remove from package and place in a bowl to cool. Once the rice is cool, stir in the salsa. Add the avocado, onion, beans, corn, cilantro, lime juice, and salt. Mix until blended. Serve chilled or at room temperature.

Options: For a spicier kick, add a seeded and diced jalapeño. For more protein, dice up one or two of TJ's Chile Lime Chicken Burgers (found in the refrigerated section), then add to the salad.

Makes 3-4 servings

Green figs and even black figs are seasonal items at Trader Joe's, so if you want to make this salad out of season, substitute pears or apples.

TURKISH SALAD
with Pomegranate Vinaigrette

¾ bag TJ's Baby Spring Mix

2-3 radishes, sliced thin

5 fresh green figs (or black figs in season)

2-3 tablespoons crumbled goat cheese

5 dried apricots, diced

3 tablespoons pistachios (raw or roasted, salted is fine)

Turkish Salad

Combine all ingredients in a medium bowl and set aside.

¾ cup TJ's Pomegranate Vinegar

4 tablespoons TJ's Extra Virgin California Estate Olive Oil

2 tablespoons TJ's Hot & Sweet Mustard

2 tablespoons TJ's Organic Blue Agave Sweetener

2 cloves of peeled garlic, minced

black pepper

Pomegranate Vinaigrette

Makes enough for 1 large salad

Whisk ingredients together, adjusting amounts for desired taste. Drizzle ¼ cup of dressing on the salad and toss. Serve immediately.

Makes 2 servings

Broccolini is such is a simple vegetable with so much flavor. The Everyday Seasoning at Trader Joe's comes with its own grinder and offers a nice fresh aroma to the coriander, mustard seeds, and other spices in the mix.

ROASTED BROCCOLINI
with Everyday Seasoning

1 package of broccolini

1 drizzle of olive oil

TJ's Everyday Seasoning to taste

Preheat oven to 400°F.

Place broccolini in a bowl with a drizzle of olive oil. Generously add Everyday Seasoning. Transfer to a 9 x 12 casserole dish or baking sheet lined with parchment paper. Roast 13–15 minutes, or until the edges are browned.

Makes 6 servings

Not only is the Sprouted Red Jasmine Rice convenient, since it comes fully cooked, but it has a wonderful slightly nutty and sweet flavor. It also has a nice chewy texture and comes with the bran intact and sprouted, which provides more nutrients.

CRISPY ASIAN SALAD
with Peanut Dressing

1 pouch TJ's Sprouted Red Jasmine Rice (in the freezer case)

1½ cups TJ's Asian Style Spicy Peanut Vinaigrette Dressing (in the refrigerated case)

2 teaspoons TJ's Toasted Sesame Oil

a dash of cayenne pepper

2 cups shredded carrots

1 package TJ's Organic Broccoli Slaw

2½ cups fresh sugar snap peas, chopped

½ cup slivered almonds or roasted peanuts

Cook the rice according to package instructions and set aside to cool.

In a large bowl, combine the dressing, oil, and cayenne pepper. Add the carrots, Broccoli Slaw, peas, peanuts, and rice. Stir to coat all ingredients with the dressing.

Optional: Add ½ cup cilantro, chopped, and a can of mandarin oranges, drained.

Makes 2-3 servings

This a great salad you can whip up during a busy work week. It's convenient, and it tastes amazing. If you create a meal plan, include this to use up leftover cooked chicken. If you don't have leftover chicken, no problem. Use Trader Joe's Just Chicken, which is fully cooked and ready to add to any recipe.

LEFTOVER CHICKEN SALAD

1½ cups butternut squash, kabocha squash, or sweet potatoes, roasted

1 package arugula greens

2 cups chicken, diced

3-4 TJ's Steamed & Peeled Baby Beets, sliced

Instructions for roasting the squash can be found on page 18. For the recipe on roasting sweet potatoes, see page 208.

Mix roasted squash or sweet potatoes, arugula, chicken, and beets together in a large bowl. Set aside.

½ cup white balsamic vinegar

3 tablespoons TJ's Sicilian Extra Virgin Olive Oil

2 garlic cloves, smashed and minced

1 teaspoon TJ's Hot & Sweet Mustard

White Balsamic Vinaigrette

Makes enough for 2 salads.

Whisk vinegar, oil, garlic, and mustard together in a small bowl. Dress the salad and serve immediately.

Note: For a more peppery, garlicky kick, make the dressing an hour ahead.

chapter 3

Kidding Around

Simple, healthy meal solutions and snacks for even the pickiest kids.

Makes 6 Roll-ups

Some kids simply love to eat vegetables, while others are more choosy.
This is a fun way to get them inter-
ested in both beets and zucchini. Shhh,
don't tell them there's beans in there
too! If the roll-ups are too hard for a
younger child, just serve the chopped
veggies with the hummus as a dip.

ZUCCHINI AND BEET
Hummus Roll-ups

2–3 zucchinis

1 tub TJ's Beet Hummus

With a mandolin or sharp knife, slice zucchini into thin
ribbon strips lengthwise. Place strips on a shallow,
microwavable dish filled with ½ inch of water. Cover
with a paper towel and microwave 1–2 minutes to soften
zucchini. Once the zucchini is soft, drain the water from
the dish and allow zucchini to cool.

Roll up the strips of zucchini, leaving the center open.
Insert a toothpick through the center to hold zucchini roll
together. Using a small spoon, add the hummus to the
center of the zucchini.

Pick up by the toothpick and pop in your mouth!

Makes 4-6 servings

If you have a sweet tooth, you will love Trader Joe's Nothing But . . . Banana, Flattened slices. They're great with peanut butter as an afternoon snack. And these roll-ups are much healthier than peanut butter and jelly sandwiches.

BANANA DATE ROLL-UPS

1 package TJ's Nothing But
   . . . Banana, Flattened
   slices
1 package TJ's Fancy Medjool
   Dates, sliced with pit removed

Peel apart and separate the flattened banana slices. Wrap each banana slice around a date. Keep wrap together by sticking a toothpick through the center. Enjoy!

Makes 6 servings

Spinach and Kale Greek Yogurt Dip has very few calories and lots of flavor. It's great in romaine lettuce wraps, on sandwiches, and as a dip.

SPINACH AND KALE DIP
with Veggies

1 container TJ's Spinach & Kale Greek Yogurt Dip

1-2 sweet red bell peppers, sliced

1 zucchini, sliced wide for dipping

1 yellow squash, sliced wide for dipping

5-6 baby carrots

Place dip in a small bowl and surround it with the sliced vegetables on a plate. Dip in!

Everyone in the family will enjoy this meal and, with a lot less sodium and fat, it's a healthier version of the Philly cheesesteak. Using the Quick to Cook Very Thinly Sliced Beef Sirloin from Trader Joe's, you get 24 grams of protein. By using European-style whole grain bread you'll add more vitamins, minerals, and fiber, as opposed to a big white bun that's been stripped of bran and nutrients.

Costa Mesa
CHEESESTEAK

½ package TJ's Fire Roasted Bell Peppers and Onions (in the freezer case)

olive oil

1 package TJ's Quick to Cook Very Thinly Sliced Beef Sirloin

3 teaspoons TJ's BBQ Rub and Seasoning with Coffee and Garlic

1 slice per serving of TJ's European Style Whole Grain Bread

2 teaspoons TJ's Fancy Shredded Lite Mexican Blend cheese

Thaw the peppers and onions according to package instructions.

Put a drizzle of olive oil in a skillet over medium heat and brown the shaved beef, approximately 8–9 minutes. Add in the rub and seasoning, and peppers and onions. Taste and add salt or additional seasoning if desired.

Top bread with the beef mixture. Sprinkle with a few teaspoons of cheese and microwave bread until the cheese is melted. If you prefer, place the whole open-faced sandwich in a 400°F preheated oven to heat.

Option: Serve with a side of TJ's Julienned Root Vegetables (in the freezer case). Follow package instructions to cook.

Tip: Use some of the beef leftovers to make the Grilled Shaved Beef Flatbread recipe on page 116.

Makes 4 servings

The colorful peppers in this recipe are crispy, sweet, and full of protein. And they make the cutest little boats! Have some fun with the kids making flags for the boats. You can even change up the recipe by using salmon instead of tuna.

TUNA BOATS

1 can TJ's Albacore Tuna in Water, Salt Added, drained

2 teaspoons organic mayonnaise

2 teaspoons plain nonfat Greek-style yogurt (any kind)

½ teaspoon garlic powder

1 teaspoon lemon juice

Himalayan pink salt

fresh cracked pepper

6-7 baby bell peppers

Mix together the tuna, mayonnaise, yogurt, garlic powder, and lemon juice in a medium bowl. Add salt and pepper to taste. Set aside.

Slice the edge lengthwise off of each pepper. Remove the seeds and discard. Fill with tuna mixture. Add a fun flag with a toothpick. Set sail on a taste adventure!

Each Clif Bar makes 3 bites

These **yummy** chocolate treats are packed with macronutrients and healthy ingredients, but they taste heavenly. The **Super Seed Blend with Cranberry & Coconut Chips** adds a little bit of crunch and a whole lot of punch. Loaded with hemp seeds, coconut chips, chia seeds, and cranberries. It provides lots of omega-3 fatty acids. These super bites will be a hit with kids and grownups alike!

CHOCOLATE BITES
with Super Seed Sprinkles

1 Chocolate Brownie Kids Clif Bar

2½ teaspoons peanut butter

2 tablespoons Super Seed Blend with Cranberry & Coconut Chips

Cut the Clif Bar into 3 pieces. Place ½ teaspoon of peanut butter on each piece. Top a piece of the bar with peanut butter. Place the pieces on a plate and sprinkle with the Super Seed blend.

Makes 3-5 servings

This is a great way to get kids to enjoy a serving of whole grains in a meal, plus it adds a lot of taste and crunch without the grease usually found in fast food or some store-bought chicken nuggets. They're great for parents too.

BAKED CHICKEN NUGGETS
with Flax Plus Multibran Flakes

2 eggs

3 skinless, boneless chicken breasts

2 cups Nature's Path Flax Plus Multibran Flakes

3-4 teaspoons TJ's 21 Seasoning Salute

½ teaspoon lemon zest

Himalayan pink salt

pepper

cooking oil

Preheat oven to 350°F.

Whisk eggs and set aside.

Rinse the chicken, pat dry and cut into 2-inch chunks.

Place cereal in a resealable plastic bag and roll into fine crumbs with a rolling pin. Pour crumbs into a bowl. Add the 21 Seasoning Salute and lemon zest, then add salt and pepper to taste.

Using tongs, dip each chicken piece into the egg, and then carefully dip each piece into the cereal mixture. Place the coated pieces on a baking sheet lined with parchment paper. Spray the tops of the nuggets with cooking oil.

Bake 6–8 minutes, until nuggets reach an internal temperature of 165°F.

Serve with TJ's Hot & Sweet Mustard, Organic Ketchup, Cilantro Salad Dressing, or Tzatziki sauce. Tzatziki sauce is a low-fat yogurt and cucumber dip that contains protein. It's a great substitute for ranch dressing when you want something creamy. Look for it in the refrigerated case.

Makes 4 servings

This snack is healthier than candy, but it tastes just as good! The naturally occurring sugars from the dates make this a winner for those with a sweet tooth. The Super Seed Blend with Cranberry and Coconut Chips also has chia seeds, buckwheat, and shelled hemp seeds. It's also great on oatmeal and mixed into muffins. It adds 5 grams of dietary fiber and 1 gram of omega-3 fatty acids per serving.

DATE SNACK

6 tablespoons organic smooth peanut butter

12 TJ's Fancy Medjool Dates, sliced and pit removed

5 teaspoons Super Seed Blend with Cranberry & Coconut Chips

Put ½ teaspoon of peanut butter on each date. Place on a plate and sprinkle the Super Seed Blend over the top. Press some of the seed mixture into the peanut butter. For a sweet and salty combination, add Inner Peas (Sugar Snap Pea Crisps) to your snack plate.

Tip: Having kids over for a slumber party? Use sunflower seed butter instead of peanut butter to make this snack more allergy friendly.

Makes 4-6 servings, depending on the size of the squash

Delicata squash have a soft skin and do not need to be peeled like butternut squash. You can eat them with the skins on! Delicata squash are native to North and South America. Although they resemble winter squash, they're more closely related to summer squash, but with a slightly nuttier flavor.

DELICATA SQUASH
Turkey "Tacos"

2-3 delicata squash

olive oil

Himalayan pink salt

pepper

2 tablespoons sunflower seed oil or olive oil

¾ pound ground turkey

2 tablespoons tomato paste or ketchup

½ package TJ's Fire Roasted Bell Peppers and Onions (from the freezer case), thawed

½ package TJ's Taco Seasoning Mix

½ teaspoon garlic powder

Preheat oven 425°F.

Slice squash lengthwise into 4 pieces and remove seeds with a spoon. Spray or drizzle olive oil on the flesh side. Add a little salt and pepper, and then place in a parchment-lined baking dish, flesh side down. Bake 20–25 minutes or until a fork easily pierces the skin.

In a skillet, over medium high heat, heat 2 tablespoons sunflower seed oil or olive oil. Add turkey and break apart with a spatula as it cooks down. Add the tomato paste, peppers and onions, taco seasoning mix, and garlic powder. Cook 10–12 minutes, until the turkey is fully cooked.

Once the turkey mixture is cooked, fill the squash "tacos" with the mixture. Serve with a side of TJ's Roasted Corn and a salsa of your choice.

Options: You can top these "tacos" with TJ's Fancy Shredded Lite Mexican Blend cheese and diced avocado.

Makes 12 1-inch meatballs

The grass-fed angus beef found in the freezer case at Trader Joe's is great. I snuck some spinach into the meatballs, so the kids get two servings of veggies!

MEATBALLS with Spinach on Zucchini "Spaghetti"

1 pound grass-fed angus beef

2 cloves of garlic, smashed and minced

1 tablespoon tomato paste or ketchup

½ medium onion, chopped

1 egg, beaten

1-2 teaspoons sunflower seed or olive oil

1 piece of TJ's European Style Whole Grain Bread, crumbled

½ cup grated Parmesan cheese

2 tablespoons fresh parsley, chopped

2 teaspoons dried oregano

1 package frozen spinach, thawed with excess liquid removed

a few dashes of salt and pepper

3 tablespoons cooking oil

1 jar TJ's Arrabiata Sauce

2-3 medium zucchinis

For the Meatballs

Mix together the beef, garlic, tomato paste, onion, egg, oil, bread, Parmesan cheese, parsley, oregano, spinach, salt, and pepper. Roll mixture into 1-inch meatballs.

Heat 3 tablespoons of cooking oil in a skillet over medium heat. Add meatballs, being careful not to overcrowd the skillet. Cook meatballs 10–12 minutes, turning several times so they brown on all sides. Once the meatballs are browned, place them on a paper towel-lined plate to drain any excess oil. Heat the pasta sauce, add meatballs and coat with sauce.

For the Spaghetti

You'll need the Veggetti Spiral Vegetable Slicer or similar tool for this recipe.

Twist the zucchini through the Veggetti to make the "spaghetti." Place the spaghetti in a microwavable bowl with ¼ inch of water. Cover lightly and steam on high for approximately 2 minutes, until tender.

Remove zucchini from the microwave and pat dry. Place on a plate and top with the meatballs. Sprinkle on Parmesan cheese and serve.

Makes 2 servings

Someone at our store accidentally ordered an abundance of spaghetti squash, so we received nine cases one day. My team told me I needed to sell it. I took it as a personal challenge and sold all nine cases in just under six hours. Customers were happy to learn how diverse and easy to cook it is.

SPAGHETTI SQUASH
with Heirloom Tomatoes

1 spaghetti squash

cooking spray

Himalayan pink salt

½ container TJ's Mini Heirloom Tomatoes, left whole or sliced in half

2 teaspoons butter or ghee

1 teaspoon TJ's Sicilian Extra Virgin Olive Oil

4 tablespoons shaved Parmesan cheese

fresh basil leaves, roughly chopped

Preheat oven to 425°F.

Carefully pierce the skin of the spaghetti squash with a sharp knife and cut in half lengthwise. Scoop out the seeds and discard. Spray the squash flesh with cooking spray and season with salt. Place flesh side down on a parchment-lined baking dish. Bake 50 minutes, or until fork tender.

Once squash is tender, remove from oven. Fluff the flesh with a fork. It will flake off from the skin and should be easy to remove.

Place in a bowl and toss with tomatoes, butter, olive oil, Parmesan cheese, and basil. Portion out and serve immediately.

Note: Spaghetti squash is a great substitute for pasta. Here's why: 1 cup of spaghetti squash has about 31 calories and only 7 grams of carbs, while pasta has 131 calories and 25 grams of carbs. Not to mention that spaghetti squash is loaded with fiber and potassium.

Makes 1 serving

Flatbread pizza is a great way to have that satisfying pizza flavor without a lot of extra carbs from a thick crust (Have your pizza and eat it too). Since you're preparing it yourself, you control how much cheese goes on the pizza.

FLATBREAD PIZZA
with Roasted Vegetables and Goat Cheese

1 TJ's Whole Grain Tortilla with rolled oats and flax seeds

1-2 teaspoons olive oil or cooking spray

3-4 slices TJ's Misto alla Griglia Marinated Grilled Eggplant & Zucchini (in the freezer case), slightly thawed

10-12 TJ's Julienne Style Sun Dried Tomatoes in Olive Oil

2 tablespoons crumbled goat cheese

a few sprinkles of grated Parmesan cheese

a pinch of fresh red pepper flakes

2-3 leaves fresh basil, roughly chopped

Preheat oven to 400°F.

Place tortilla on a baking sheet. Coat the top with a little olive oil and bake until slightly golden and crunchy. Immediately remove tortilla from the oven. Add the eggplant and zucchini, tomatoes, cheeses, and red pepper. Bake 5–7 minutes, or until cheese just begins to melt and vegetables are warm. Remove and add basil. Serve immediately.

Options: Topping choices are certainly endless with pizza, but I often add diced, pitted Kalamata olives or mozzarella cheese pearls.

chapter 4

It's a Wrap!

Enough wraps to keep your taste buds happy all week.

Makes 4 servings

Trader Joe's just began carrying thin cedar wraps for baking or grilling food. Why use them? Because they infuse a nice flavor and keep the items inside super moist. Plus, they make cooking fish easy, and make for a great presentation at a party.

CEDAR-WRAPPED SALMON

4-5 cedar grilling wraps, cut in half

1 package TJ's Wild Silver Coho Salmon, deboned, skinless, thawed

¼ cup TJ's Soyaki Sauce

a pinch of fresh cracked black pepper

3-4 TJ's Organic Carrots of Many Colors, peeled and cut into thin, 4-inch-long strips

3 green onions, cut into 4-inch-long strips

Preheat oven to 400°F.

Soak cedar wraps and included twine in water for 10 minutes. Place a cup of water on top of the wraps to keep them submerged.

Use a paper towel to pat dry the thawed salmon, then cut into 3-inch-long chunks. Place the fish in a bowl with the Soyaki Sauce and add the pepper. Allow to marinate for 10 to 30 minutes.

Line a baking sheet with parchment paper and place cedar wraps on top. Place a piece of fish and a few onion and carrot strips on each wrap. Top with ½ teaspoon of Soyaki Sauce. Roll up each wrap parallel to the grain and tie together using the twine.

Bake for 6-9 minutes, until fish is firm and opaque. Remove from oven and place directly on plate to serve.

Note: You can grill these outside. Place the wraps directly onto grill rack and cook medium-high (about 450°F) with lid closed for 3-4 minutes on each side. This gives the wraps an extra punch of flavor.

Makes 5 servings

These succulent, sweet, and tangy wraps also work great with The TJ Extra Large Black Raisins. They may look strange, but they are super sweet and delicious.

CURRIED CHICKEN SALAD
Lettuce Wraps

1 package TJ's Curry Chicken Tenders (in the refrigerated case)

1 cup dried cranberries or TJ's Organic Thompson Seedless Raisins

¼ cup slivered almonds

1 granny smith apple, skin on, diced

¼ cup plain, nonfat, Greek-style yogurt

¼ cup organic mayonnaise

2 teaspoons apple cider vinegar

a few dashes of curry powder

½ package romaine hearts

Preheat oven to 400°F.

Bake tenders on a parchment paper-lined baking sheet for approximately 8 minutes, until they reach an internal temperature of 165°F. Allow tenders to cool. Once they're cooled, dice the nuggets.

While the chicken cools, mix together the cranberries or raisins, almonds, apple, yogurt, mayonnaise, and vinegar. Add extra curry powder if desired. Once the chicken is cool, add it to the mixture, and then place in the refrigerator to chill.

Scoop salad into romaine lettuce hearts and serve.

Makes 2 servings

Chicken is one of those lean proteins you can do 1,000 things with using all kinds of seasonings from Trader Joe's. Using the fully cooked Just Chicken (in the refrigerator case) is amazing for meals on the fly. Skinless chicken breasts have less fat and pack a full 24 grams of lean protein in a 3-ounce serving.

FAST MEXICAN WRAP
with Chicken

1 cup TJ's Just Chicken, diced

¼ cup plain, nonfat, Greek-style yogurt

¼ cup organic mayonnaise

¼ cup cilantro, roughly chopped

a few dashes of Himalayan pink salt

1½ cups shredded cabbage or TJ's Cruciferous Crunch Collection

½ of a small Ataulfo mango (or any ripe mango), skinned and diced

½ cup spicy hummus or red pepper hummus

2 tortillas

lime wedges

Dice chicken. Mix together the yogurt, mayonnaise, cilantro, and salt. Add the cabbage, mango, and chicken, stirring until combined.

Spread hummus on the tortilla. Top with the chicken mixture. If desired, add a squirt of lime juice. Serve open faced or rolled up.

Note: Vegetarians can substitute TJ's Chicken-Less Strips for this recipe (prepare according to package instructions). They have 20 grams of lean protein per serving and zero cholesterol.

Makes 4 flatbreads cut into
2 pieces (as shown)

Using the leftover filling from the Costa Mesa Cheesesteak on page 90, you can enjoy another satisfying, low-carb meal. By using a tortilla instead of a thick bun you save a few grams of carbs, yet still get that cheesesteak flavor you crave with a Costa Mesa twist. I've suggested the Whole Wheat Lavash Bread, because it doesn't contain preservatives.

GRILLED SHAVED BEEF
Flatbread

1 piece TJ's Whole Wheat
   Lavash Bread
Costa Mesa Cheesesteak filling
   (see the recipe on page 90)
Coconut oil cooking spray
a handful of TJ's Fancy Shredded
   Lite Mexican Blend cheese

Coat a griddle with the cooking spray, then heat it on the stove over high heat.

Cut Lavash bread into 4 x 8-inch pieces. On one side of the bread, add the cheesesteak mixture and cheese blend. Fold the empty half over the filling and cook directly on the griddle. Press down flatbread firmly with a metal spatula to sear the sandwich. Reduce heat to medium. Cover sandwich with a small piece of aluminum foil or a saucepan lid to retain heat. Cook each side approximately 3 minutes, until cheese has melted. Serve immediately.

Option: Serve these with TJ's Inner Peas Snack on the side. They satisfy that salty, crunchy urge and are healthier than potato chips.

Makes 2-3 servings

I sometimes call this recipe "Curry in a Hurry." It's made with Ataulfo mangoes, which are often referred to as the champagne of mangoes. They're small and have a very thin, flat seed inside. They're available at Trader Joe's for about three weeks while in season, then they're gone like the wind. Get them while you can. Unlike their larger cousin, these mangoes are creamy and have smooth fruit.

CURRIED CHICKEN
Flatbread

4 teaspoons red onion, minced

1 small Ataulfo mango (or any ripe mango), skinned and diced

¼ cup TJ's Masala Simmer Sauce

a shake or two of cayenne pepper

1 tablespoon plain, nonfat Greek-style yogurt (optional)

¼ cup cilantro, roughly cut

1 cup TJ's Just Chicken, diced

½ red bell pepper, diced

2-4 butter lettuce leaves or romaine lettuce

2 whole wheat organic tortillas

Combine onion, mango, sauce, cayenne pepper, yogurt, and cilantro in a bowl. Then, add chicken and red bell pepper. Stir to coat the chicken. Place on the lettuce leaves, roll into a flat tortilla, and enjoy.

Option: If you have any cooked sweet potatoes, dice and add them to the mixture.

The Roasted Red Pepper Spread with Eggplant and Garlic is a great substitute for mayonnaise on this roll-up. To add variety to this recipe, try it with romaine hearts and other types of TJ sandwich meats.

Turkey, Grilled Eggplant, and ZUCCHINI ROLL-UP

a few pieces of TJ's Misto alla Griglia Marinated Grilled Eggplant & Zucchini (freezer case)

whole wheat tortillas (1 per roll-up)

2 tablespoons TJ's Roasted Red Pepper Spread with Eggplant and Garlic

2 slices smoked turkey

Set your microwave to defrost and thaw only the amount of grilled eggplant and zucchini you plan to eat.

Lay each tortilla on a plate, add the spread, top with turkey and vegetables. Roll up the tortilla, slice in half, and enjoy.

Makes 1 serving

There's more than 40,000 kinds of rice in the world. Trader Joe's has quite a good selection, which includes black rice, wild rice, red rice, sprouted rice, and quite a few fully cooked organic varieties. The black rice that looks somewhat purple when cooked has a delicious nutty taste. Make extra and freeze it in resealable plastic bags to toss into soups or stir-fries.

CHICKEN WRAP with Black Rice and Spicy Hummus

½ cup black rice

vegetable broth

¾ cup TJ's Just Chicken

1 teaspoon roasted, salted pistachios

1 tablespoon chopped cilantro

1 TJ's Whole Grain Flour Tortilla with Flaxseeds

3 tablespoons TJ's Smooth and Creamy Spicy Hummus

Cook black rice according to package instructions. I like cooking it in vegetable broth. Check the water level while it's cooking, as it can lose moisture too fast. Add more liquid as necessary. Once cooked, allow rice to cool down to room temperature. Toss chicken, pistachios, and cilantro into rice.

Place the tortilla on a plate and spread on the hummus. Add the chicken and rice mixture on top. Serve flat or roll up and enjoy.

chapter

5

One-Pot Wonders

Easy, single-pot meals you can make for the whole family.

Makes 3-4 servings

This is a great, easy-to-prepare dish for a hearty fall dinner with the whole family. It's rustic and so simple! I often shy away from the prepackaged seasoned vegetable side dishes at Trader Joe's, because they're often high in sodium or calories. But I make an exception for this recipe. This meal is so simple, yet so yumbalicious!

AHI TUNA
with Fire-Roasted Vegetables with Balsamic Butter Sauce

1 package (about 1 pound) TJ's Ahi Tuna

1 package TJ's Fire Roasted Vegetables with Balsamic Butter Sauce (from the freezer case), thawed slightly

2 tablespoons olive oil

Thaw fish for approximately 20 minutes in cold water. Once thawed, remove from packaging and pat dry.

Add olive oil to a large skillet and heat over medium heat. Add the contents of the fire-roasted veggies package, including the frozen butter sauce pellets. Cook 3–4 minutes, stirring occasionally, then turn off heat.

Warm a griddle over high heat. Once hot, carefully spray the inside of the pan with canola spray or a little coconut cooking spray. Add the tuna fillets and sear on both sides, approximately 3 minutes per side. Transfer the fish to the skillet with the vegetables and sauce. Cover and continue to cook on medium heat until fish is fully cooked through, approximately 4–6 minutes. Serve immediately.

Option: Serve atop TJ's Rice Medley. This delicious medley includes brown rice, red rice, and black barley. Follow package instructions for cooking.

Makes 4-5 servings

This is one of my favorite recipes! Trader Joe's has a good Cioppino Seafood Stew, which is similar, but I prefer making my own so I can control the sodium and seasonings a bit more. This stew is great to share with the family during the holiday festivities or to cozy up a rainy day at home.

SEAFOOD STEW

3 teaspoons of TJ's Sicilian Extra Virgin Olive Oil

8-10 garlic cloves, smashed and minced

1 shallot, chopped

1 can Cento San Marzano Peeled Tomatoes

1 cup vegetable broth

2 bay leaves

1 cup TJ's "Two Buck Chuck" Chardonnay*

¼ teaspoon thyme, dried or fresh

a few shakes of cayenne pepper

Himalayan pink salt

¼ teaspoon fresh cracked pepper

4-5 strands of saffron

1 package TJ's Boneless Skinless Alaskan Cod Pieces, thawed

1 tablespoon butter

1-pound box TJ's Steamer Clams

10-14 raw shrimp, tails on, thawed

1 lemon, juiced

In a large skillet or deep saucepan, heat olive oil, garlic, and shallot over medium heat. Cook until garlic and shallots are golden. Add tomatoes and cut them in half in the pan with a knife or kitchen scissors. Add vegetable broth, bay leaves, wine, thyme, cayenne pepper, salt, pepper, and saffron. Stir until combined. Then, add the cod and butter. Cover the pan and cook on low–medium heat for 10 minutes.

In the microwave, heat clams according to package instructions and set aside.

Add the shrimp to the stew, cover, and cook for an additional 5–8 minutes over low–medium heat. Add in the clams with shells, and remember to add the juice from the clams. Stir in gently. Taste and adjust seasoning as desired. Add lemon juice and serve immediately.

Option: This stew can be served over brown rice or quinoa pasta. I like TJ's Organic Brown Rice, which is located in the freezer case.

*Note: Not all Trader Joe's carry alcoholic beverages. TJ's "Two Buck Chuck" Chardonnay refers to their famously low-cost Charles Shaw wine. Look for any low cost chardonnay.

Makes 4-5 servings

This is a vegan meal even meat lovers will savor. The curry flavoring makes this dish hearty and comforting. The best thing is there's no right or wrong way to make it. If you have other vegetables in the fridge, add them in. The more the merrier! For a variation, try using organic tempeh. Simply dice it into cubes and add it after the onions are cooked. It's a nutty, hearty, protein-rich addition.

THAI RED CURRY with Vegetables and Garbanzo Beans

2 teaspoons coconut oil or olive oil

½ teaspoon fresh ginger, grated

2-3 cloves garlic, smashed and minced

½ cup red onion, sliced largely

½ red bell pepper, chopped

1 bottle TJ's Thai Red Curry Sauce

1 can organic garbanzo beans, rinsed and drained

1½ cups fresh broccoli florets

1½ cups organic sugar snap peas, cut in half

1 teaspoon coconut sugar

a dash of cayenne pepper

1 pouch TJ's Organic Brown Rice

3-4 lime wedges

Pour coconut oil into a skillet and cook ginger and garlic for 1 minute over medium heat. Add in the onion and red bell pepper. Cook approximately 3 minutes, or until the onion is slightly translucent. Add the sauce, beans, broccoli, snap peas, sugar, and cayenne pepper. Simmer on low–medium heat for 8–10 minutes, until the vegetables are cooked to your desired preference. I like them cooked but still crunchy.

Cook rice in the microwave according to package instructions. Once rice is cooked, add it to the skillet and stir in.

Squeeze on some fresh lime juice and serve.

Note: For an extra creamy consistency, add ½ cup of coconut milk (including some of the solids).

Makes 3 servings

This recipe includes a combination of three main ingredients that most family members enjoy. Add a touch of marsala wine and a touch of zest from the Parmesan and you've just elevated this dish to a nice rustic meal. No need for a heavy cream sauce.

CHICKEN WITH MUSHROOM MEDLEY and French Green Beans

1 package TJ's Mushroom Medley, thawed

a few drops of olive oil

⅓ cup water

2 fresh, boneless, skinless chicken breasts, cut into thirds

3 tablespoons sherry or marsala wine

2 cups TJ's French Green Beans (in the freezer section), slightly thawed

handful of TJ's Shaved Parmesan Reggiano Cheese

a pinch of fresh cracked black pepper

Himalayan pink salt

Empty the package of Mushroom Medley into a large skillet with a few drops of olive oil and cook over medium heat. Add water, chicken, and sherry or wine. Stir, cover, and then let simmer on low–medium heat for 6–8 minutes, until chicken is cooked through.

Put the green beans in a microwavable dish. Add 2 tablespoons of water, cover, and cook in a microwave for 4 minutes. Once the beans are done, drain the liquid and add to the skillet. Stir to coat the beans and cook for 1 minute. Top with the cheese and black pepper. Season to taste. Add Himalayan pink salt if desired.

Serve in a shallow bowl with some of the sauce.

Note: Be careful not to overcook the beans, or they'll lose their wonderful sweet taste and crisp–tender texture.

Makes 3 servings

This is an "OMG" recipe, according to my neighbor and volunteer taste tester Alysia! I've used the Grecian Style Eggplant with Tomatoes and Onions, a fairly new item in the grocery aisle, to season the chicken. The vegetables make the chicken succulent and rich with flavor. We'll have to pray to the Trader Joe's gods that they don't discontinue this item. I can't wait to play with it in other recipes.

GREEK CHICKEN
with Eggplant and Onion

3 boneless, skinless chicken breasts

1 can TJ's Grecian Style Eggplant with Tomatoes & Onions (in the grocery aisle)

½ to ¾ cup Kalamata olives, pitted and diced

3 cloves garlic, smashed and minced

1 teaspoon dried oregano

black pepper to taste

olive oil

2 zucchinis, sliced in thin discs

3-4 tablespoons crumbled feta cheese

3 teaspoons fresh basil, roughly cut

Preheat oven to 375°F.

In a Dutch oven, combine the chicken, eggplant, olives, garlic, oregano, and black pepper. Cover and cook for 25 minutes or until the chicken reaches an internal temperature of 165°F.

While the chicken is cooking, heat the olive oil in a small skillet. Toss in zucchini and cook over medium heat for 3–4 minutes, stirring often, until slightly tender. Remove from heat and set aside.

Once the chicken is done, place a chicken breast with some sauce and zucchini in a shallow bowl. Top with feta and basil. Serve immediately.

Note: The feta and olives provide enough salt to permeate the dish.

Makes 5-6 servings

A mouthwatering, super tender taste of the South. Every region in the south has its own style of BBQ sauce, and South Carolina is known for a mustard-based sauce. Use the slow cooker to get that oh-so-tender, melt-in-your-mouth pork! Once you've tasted this BBQ pork, you'll want to sing its praises with a hound in the back of a truck.

CAROLINA GOLD BBQ Lettuce Wraps with Tangy Cruciferous Slaw

1 pork loin roast, cut into thirds

1 jar TJ's Carolina Gold Barbeque Sauce

1 bay leaf, crushed (optional)

2 tablespoons apple cider vinegar

a few dashes of cayenne pepper for extra heat, if desired

½ cup water

a few dashes of salt

romaine hearts

For the Pork

Combine all ingredients, except the romaine hearts, in a slow cooker. Cover and cook on low heat 8–10 hours. Check on it once or twice while it's cooking. The meat should start to fall apart with a fork at the 10th hour! Serve with romaine hearts and top with homemade slaw.

See recipe for the Tangy Cruciferous Slaw on page 209.

Who needs to eat out when you can make Thai at home? It only takes about 20 minutes to make. The flaky, white mahi mahi is mouthwatering with these exotic spices. It smells so fragrant while cooking that your neighbors will be scrambling to your door.

THAI GREEN CURRY MAHI MAHI with
Heirloom Rainbow Carrots

1 package TJ's Mahi Mahi Fillets, thawed

½ teaspoon freshly grated ginger

Himalayan pink salt

a dash of cayenne pepper

4 garlic cloves, smashed and minced

1-2 tablespoons TJ's Organic Virgin Coconut Oil, liquefied

4 TJ's Organic Carrots of Many Colors, julienned

1½-2 cups fresh broccoli florets

1 pouch TJ's Organic Brown Rice or Sprouted Red Jasmine Rice

a pinch of fresh cilantro

¼ lemon, juiced

1 bottle TJ's Thai Green Curry Simmer Sauce

3 teaspoons lemon zest

Thaw packaged mahi mahi in cold water for 20 minutes. Remove from packaging and cut into chunks, if desired. Pat dry and place in a bowl.

In a separate bowl, combine ginger, salt, pepper, garlic, and coconut oil. Add the fish, stirring until coated. Allow it to marinate for a few minutes.

Place carrots in a microwavable bowl and add water to cover carrots. Cook on high 4–5 minutes, until tender. Drain water and set aside.

Transfer the fish and simmer sauce to a large skillet. Cover and cook on low–medium for 6 minutes, turning fish once. Add broccoli and cook 6–8 minutes. Add the carrots and 3 teaspoons of lemon zest and cook 3 more minutes, or until the veggies are tender and the fish is firm.

Serve over the rice of your choice. Add fresh cilantro for garnish and a squirt of lemon juice just before serving.

This ridiculously yummy, hearty soup provides lean protein from the chicken sausage (22 grams of protein per link) and more from the garbanzo beans. This soup is also loaded with fiber. This recipe makes a lot, y'all, so it's a perfect meal for family gatherings.

RUSTIC SOUP WITH CHICKEN
Apple Sausage and Sweet Potatoes

1 package All Natural Sweet Apple Chicken Sausage, diced and browned

1 32-ounce container TJ's Organic Vegetable Broth

1 can TJ's Diced & Fire Roasted Tomatoes

2 sweet potatoes, skins on, cut into bite-size chunks

¼ cup sweet onion, diced

½ cup TJ's Eggplant Garlic Spread

4 garlic cloves, smashed and minced

a few dashes of red pepper flakes

¼ teaspoon smoked paprika

½ package TJ's Sliced Crimini Mushrooms

1 can organic garbanzo beans, rinsed and drained

Himalayan pink salt

fresh cracked pepper

2 cups TJ's Cruciferous Crunch Collection

Heat a skillet over medium heat and toss in the diced sausage. Cook 8–9 minutes, stirring occasionally to prevent burning. Cook until browned and set aside.

In a large soup pot, combine sausage, broth, tomatoes, sweet potatoes, onion, spread, garlic, red pepper flakes, paprika, mushrooms, beans, salt, and pepper. Cook partially covered on low–medium heat for 30 minutes. Add the cruciferous mix. Stir and serve. It's even more delicious a few hours later or the next day.

Options: Try variations of this recipe. Use the fresh diced butternut squash that can be found in the refrigerator case at Trader Joe's, or use white pinto beans instead of garbanzo beans.

Makes 4 servings

Winter squash varieties have a nice nutty taste and are easy to experiment with. They're fun to stuff in fall and winter simply because they're the perfect container for grain-based warm salads. Enjoy the tastes of Thanksgiving by using TJ's Poultry Rub.

STUFFED WINTER SQUASH

1 pouch TJ's Rice Medley

4 small winter or acorn squash

canola cooking spray

Himalayan pink salt

pepper

2 teaspoons butter

¼ of red bell pepper, diced

¼ sweet onion, diced

½ teaspoon TJ's Poultry Rub

¼ cup raw pumpkin seeds

3 tablespoons shaved Parmesan cheese

1 fresh sage leaf, minced

Preheat oven to 425°F.

Cook the rice according to package instructions and set aside.

Using a small, very sharp knife, carefully cut at a slight angle around the top of each squash. Remove the top, then scoop out the seeds and fibers and discard. Spray the inside with cooking spray. Season with a little salt and pepper.

Place squash, top down, on a baking sheet lined with parchment paper. Bake 15–20 minutes. Remove the pan from the oven and turn the squash so the top is facing up. Bake 15 more minutes, or until tender.

While the squash is baking, melt the butter in a skillet. Add the peppers, onions, and poultry rub. Cook on medium for 5 minutes, or until the onion becomes soft and translucent. Add the rice, pumpkin seeds, Parmesan, and sage. Stir for several minutes.

Remove the squash from the oven and reduce oven temperature to 400°F. Stuff each squash—overstuffing is encouraged! Add more cheese or seasoning, if desired.

Return stuffed squash to the oven. Bake 18–20 minutes. Pierce a fork through the side of the squash; if it goes through easily, it's done.

Makes 5 servings

Invite the Middle East into your home with the exotic aromas of cinnamon, Tunisian lemons, and dried fruits while this is cooking. The anticipation is worth it! The prunes and cinnamon cook down to envelop the meat with a rich sweetness, while the tangy lemon and hint of mint add brightness to the palette.

A Dutch oven or heavy-duty pot that evenly distributes the heat from all sides works best for this recipe.

MOROCCAN BEEF TAGINE

1½ lbs TJ's Lean Beef Stew Meat
Himalayan pink salt
pepper
4 tablespoons whole wheat flour
olive oil
¼ onion, diced
4 cups beef broth
2 tablespoons tomato paste
  (or ketchup)
2 slices TJ's Preserved Lemon Slices
  or ¾ teaspoon fresh lime zest
8 dried apricots, chopped
5 dried prunes, chopped
1½ teaspoons cumin
1½ teaspoons ground cinnamon
½ teaspoon honey
a dash of cayenne pepper
½ teaspoon thyme, fresh or dried
⅔ cup TJ's Sprouted Organic
  California Rice
a few sprigs of fresh mint
1½ teaspoons pistachios, shelled,
  roasted, salted, chopped

Preheat oven to 350°F.

Pat the beef dry. Add salt and pepper to all sides. Put whole wheat flour on a shallow plate. Roll the meat in the flour to dust, then set aside.

Heat a few teaspoons of olive oil in a Dutch oven over medium–high heat on the stove-top. Once the oil is hot, use tongs to add the beef. Cook the beef, turning the pieces to brown all sides. Turn off stove-top once beef is done.

In a large bowl, combine onion, beef broth, tomato paste lemon, apricots, prunes, cumin, cinnamon, honey, cayenne pepper, and thyme. Mix until everything is blended together. Pour mixture into the Dutch oven. Add in the uncooked rice. Place in preheated oven, cover and cook approximately 90 minutes, stirring occasionally. Add extra water if needed. Sprinkle in ½ teaspoon diced fresh mint and 1 teaspoon of the pistachios. Cover and cook another 30 minutes.

Transfer to a nice serving dish, garnish with fresh mint and a few sprinkles of the remaining pistachios.

Makes 4-6 servings

Simply put, this is an effortless way to enjoy a succulent slow-cooked chicken chock full of smoky, spicy flavors. Green Dragon Hot Sauce is a spicy new condiment at Trader Joe's that can be added to your arsenal of hot sauces for all sorts of recipes. Paired here with the smoky Chipotle Salsa for a mighty duo.

CHIPOTLE PULLED CHICKEN

3 skinless, boneless chicken breasts

1 jar TJ's Chipotle Salsa

¼ cup TJ's Green Dragon Hot Sauce

5 cloves of garlic, smashed and minced

¼ cup fresh cilantro, roughly chopped

1 teaspoon apple cider vinegar

¼ sweet onion, chopped

½ teaspoon ground cumin

1½ cups TJ's Roasted Corn, thawed

Himalayan pink salt

pepper

1 can organic pinto beans, rinsed and drained

Combine all ingredients, except the beans, in the slow cooker. Set slow cooker for 8 hours on low. When done, the meat should pull apart easily with a fork. Mix in the beans and serve.

Note: If you want more heat, add ¼ of a seeded and diced jalapeño, or double the Green Dragon Hot Sauce.

Impress your friends with a delicious, aromatic paella dish. It can be prepared in less than an hour.

PAELLA WITH MAHI MAHI

½ package raw shelled shrimp with tails on, thawed

1 package mahi mahi, thawed and diced into 2-inch cubes

1 tablespoon olive oil

1 package Chicken Andouille Sausage, cut into ¼-inch-thick discs

6-8 peeled garlic cloves, minced

½ bag Trader Joe's Fire-Roasted Bell Peppers and Onions* thawed

1 medium-large tomato, diced

2 pouches TJ's Rice Medley*

32-ounce container TJ's Organic Chicken Broth

1.02-ounce size jar TJ's Spanish Saffron

Himalayan pink salt

fresh cracked black pepper

1-pound box TJ's Steamer Clams*

2 lemons, juiced

½ cup frozen organic peas

red chili pepper flakes, to taste

a pinch of fresh parsley, diced

lemon wedges

Thaw the shrimp and mahi mahi in cold water.

In a large skillet on medium heat, add the olive oil and sausage. Cook for 5 minutes, until sausage is browned on all sides. Add the garlic, fire-roasted vegetables, and tomato. Stir and cook for 2 minutes.

Cook the rice in the microwave according to package instructions, cooking one pouch at a time. Once it's cooked, add the rice to the skillet. Pour in 1½ cups of chicken broth and the saffron, and simmer on medium heat. Allow some of the liquid to evaporate and get absorbed by the rice. Wait 5–7 minutes, then add in salt, pepper, and 1½ cups more of the chicken broth. Next, add the mahi mahi and shrimp. Reduce heat to low–medium and cover skillet.

Cook the clams in a microwave according to package instructions. Once done, add clams, including liquid, to the skillet. Stir gently. Once the shrimp are pink and the fish is fully cooked through, incorporate lemon juice and peas. Sprinkle in salt and red chili pepper flakes to taste. Cook 2 minutes more to let peas heat through. Toss in fresh parsley and serve with ample wedges of lemon.

*Found in the freezer case.

Makes 6 servings

Super low fat, low carb, and high in flavor, this chicken is spicy with a hint of sweetness from the corn that makes this a treat for your taste buds. If you dare, add a bit more of the Green Dragon Hot Sauce on top when serving.

Slow Cooked
TOMATILLO CHICKEN

5-6 skinless, boneless chicken breasts

1 cup TJ's Chunky Salsa

1 jar TJ's Organic Tomatillo & Roasted Yellow Chili Salsa

½ jar TJ's Corn and Chile Tomato-Less Salsa

¼ TJ's Green Dragon Hot Sauce

3-4 large garlic cloves, minced

Combine all ingredients in the slow cooker. Set slow cooker on low and cook for 10 hours. The chicken should pull apart easily when done. Delicious!

chapter

6

Prep for Success

Easy meals you can divide and store in the fridge to take for lunches, or have as prepared meals for the week.

Makes 4-5 servings

Everyone loves fresh Southwestern flavors, but eating out at a restaurant can sometimes mean more calories than you need. You can make this recipe in 10 minutes, and you'll be surprised at how it tastes: crisp, flavorful, and spicy. Nothing says summer like this salad.

CALIENTE CHICKEN

2 packages TJ's All Natural Chicken Tenders

2 tablespoons TJ's California Estate Olive Oil or grape seed oil

1½ tablespoons taco seasoning

1 package romaine lettuce, pre-cut

½ cup Corn and Chile Tomato-Less Salsa

3 teaspoons TJ's Cilantro Salad Dressing (in the refrigerated case)

½ red onion, diced

10-12 grape tomatoes, diced

1 avocado, diced

several fresh cilantro leaves, diced

1 lime, cut into wedges

Place chicken tenders in a bowl and drizzle with oil. Sprinkle in the taco seasoning and mix to coat chicken.

Drizzle a little oil in a large nonstick pan and cook chicken over medium–high heat both sides are browned, approximately 4 minutes per side.

For each serving, add romaine lettuce to plate, top with 3–4 pieces of chicken, ½ cup salsa, and cilantro dressing. Add onion, tomato, avocado, and a few diced cilantro leaves for garnish. Squeeze fresh lime over food before serving.

Makes 3 servings

Trader Joe's salmon is flash frozen at sea and is really a great value. They have a good selection of wild caught varieties, including King, Coho, and Silverbrite. The BBQ sauce adds a nice smoky, sweet spice to the fish on top, while the plank provides a foolproof way to cook the fish without failure.

Cedar-Planked
COHO SALMON with BBQ Sauce

1 cedar grilling plank*

1 package TJ's Wild Coho Salmon, skinless, boneless

coconut cooking spray

½ cup TJ's Organic Sriracha and Roasted Garlic BBQ Sauce

2-3 green onions

Preheat oven to 450°F.

Soak the cedar plank in the sink for 30–60 minutes.

Thaw salmon in cold water in the sink, approximately 15 minutes. Once thawed, remove from package, rinse and pat dry with a paper towel. Coat both sides of the salmon with coconut cooking spray. Then coat both sides with the BBQ sauce and set aside.

Place cedar plank on a baking sheet and heat for 5 minutes. Place salmon on the plank, top with additional sauce, and bake approximately 30 minutes, until the fillet can be flaked with a fork. Top with diced green onions and serve immediately.

Note: Add a little water to the baking sheet to prevent extra sauce or drippings from burning.

* You can get cedar planks at most grocery stores near the seafood counter or in the kitchen tools aisle.

Makes 6 servings

This recipe consists of Hot & Sweet Chili Jam with beef. I know, I know, sounds weird, right? But you have to try it. The sweet roasted peppers and onions round it out nicely! These lettuce wraps are perfect for a picnic or lunchtime snack.

Spicy Hot Sweet
SIRLOIN LETTUCE WRAPS

2 teaspoons sunflower seed oil or olive oil

1 package shaved beef

3-4 garlic cloves, smashed and minced

3-4 tablespoons TJ's Hot & Sweet Chili Jam (more or less based on desired heat)

½ package TJ's Fire Roasted Peppers and Onions, thawed

3 romaine lettuce hearts

1 pouch TJ's Organic Brown Rice, cook according to directions on package

Drizzle a little oil into a skillet over medium–high heat and rapidly cook the shaved beef. After 2 minutes, add the garlic, chili jam, and peppers and onions. Reduce heat to medium and break apart the beef as you stir. Once browned, remove from heat.

Arrange 1 or 2 romaine lettuce leaves on a plate and fill with beef mixture. Serve with rice and a little extra Hot & Sweet Chili Jam on the side, or top with a little of TJ's Sriracha and Roasted Garlic BBQ Sauce.

Makes 4-5 servings

Any carnivore will cherish this salad that's effortless to make. The Santa Maria Boneless Beef Tri-Tip Roast at Trader Joe's is fabulously seasoned and ready for the grill or roasting in the oven. You want to be careful how much of this beef you eat, since it's a tad high in sodium. For a nice side dish, pair with the Murasaki Sweet Potatoes with Sriracha and Roasted Garlic BBQ Sauce on page 164!

TRI-TIP ROAST SALAD
with Roasted Tomatillo Salsa

1 Santa Maria Marinated Boneless Beef Tri-Tip Roast (packages sold by weight)

1 package romaine lettuce

1 container TJ's Roasted Tomatillo Salsa (refrigerator case)

2-3 teaspoons per serving TJ's Corn and Chile Tomato-less Salsa

Preheat oven to 425°F.

Place roast on a baking sheet and roast 30–40 minutes for rare cooked beef, and 40–45 minutes for medium-rare.

Remove from oven and check temperature with a meat thermometer. It should read around 135°F for medium-rare, and 150°F for medium doneness. Allow to rest with a piece of tinfoil loosely over the top. The meat will continue to cook for a few minutes.

Once cooked to desired temperature, cut beef into thin pieces against the grain. Arrange meat on romaine lettuce leaves, top with the salsa and a small side of corn and chili salsa. Serve right away. The meat is also good cold!

Makes 5 servings

Murasaki means "purple" in Japanese. These sweet potatoes from Japan have a wonderful nutty taste and creamy texture, and are delightful with hot sauce on top! They make a good complex carb afternoon snack or a great side dish.

MURASAKI SWEET POTATOES
with Sriracha and Roasted Garlic BBQ Sauce

3 Murasaki sweet potatoes, cut in half width-wise; then sliced in ¼-inch pieces

canola or coconut oil cooking spray

½ teaspoon TJ's Sriracha and Roasted Garlic BBQ Sauce per slice of potato

Himalayan pink salt

1 spring onion, diced (optional)

Preheat oven to 375°F.

Scrub and rinse sweet potato pieces with skin on. Place potatoes on parchment paper-lined baking sheet. Spray potatoes with canola or coconut oil, and then coat with the sauce. Bake 12–14 minutes or until tender. Sprinkle with salt and onion. Serve hot.

Makes 12 servings

Spiedies originated in New York State and are usually served in a sandwich. I think they're great as is. Or use flatbread instead of a big bun, to save a few calories. Try serving them with a little tzatziki.

CHICKEN SPIEDIES

½ cup sherry

¼ cup extra virgin olive oil

¼ cup shallots, minced

3 large cloves of garlic, minced

1 tablespoon, fresh flat-leaf parsley, minced

2 bay leaves, crumbled

1 teaspoon dried oregano

1 teaspoon dried thyme

⅛ teaspoon red chili pepper flakes

⅛ teaspoon ground white pepper

sea salt, kosher salt, or pink salt

⅓ cup water

¼ cup purple onion

2 tablespoons red wine vinegar

2 tablespoons white balsamic vinegar

1½–2 pounds chicken tenders, or skinless, boneless chicken breasts sliced into strips

12-inch wooden skewers, soaked in water for 30 minutes prior to grilling

For the Marinade

Combine the sherry, olive oil, shallots, garlic, parsley, bay leaves, oregano, thyme, chili pepper flakes, white pepper, salt, water, onion, and vinegars in a large bowl and mix well. Add the chicken. Cover and marinate in the refrigerator for at least 4 hours. For more intense flavor allow chicken to marinate overnight.

Grilling the Chicken

Remove the chicken from the refrigerator 15 minutes before it's time to grill.

Preheat the gas grill on high with lid closed. If you're using a charcoal grill, prepare for direct heat cooking over hot charcoal.

While the grill is heating up, put the chicken pieces onto the skewers.

If you're using a gas grill, reduce the heat to medium. Carefully coat the grill surface with cooking spray, spraying at an angle. Also lightly spray the chicken skewers on both sides. Place the skewers directly on the grill. Keep the grill lid open, as these will cook very quickly. Cook approximately 5 minutes on each side, turning once. They're done once the internal temperature reaches 165°F. Remove from the grill and set on a plate.

Option: Serve with grilled fresh tomatoes. Simply cut tomatoes in half, add a little olive oil and grill them for a few minutes on each side. Add salt and fresh black pepper to taste.

Makes 6 servings

This is a wonderfully light salad you can indulge in any time of the year. Packed with crunch, lean protein, and fiber.

LENTIL SALAD
with Sugar Snaps and Balsamic Vinaigrette

1 package TJ's Steamed Lentils (in the produce refrigerated section)

1 package TJ's Mini Heirloom Tomatoes

½ cup balsamic vinaigrette

½ bag TJ's Organic Sugar Snap Peas, cut in half

fresh cracked black pepper

Himalayan pink salt

5-6 fresh basil leaves, roughly cut

½ container TJ's Crumbled Goat Cheese

Gently mix lentils, tomatoes, vinaigrette, snap peas, pepper, salt and basil together. Taste and add more vinaigrette or other seasoning if desired. Add the goat cheese and carefully stir it in, but not too much, or it will become gray.

Option: For a variation, use crumbled feta cheese.

Makes 3 servings

CHICKEN ENCRUSTED
with Flax Plus Multibran Flakes

3 skinless, boneless chicken breasts

2 cups Nature's Path Flax Plus Multibran Flakes

3-4 teaspoons TJ's 21 Seasoning Salute

½ teaspoon lemon zest

Himalayan pink salt

Fresh cracked pepper

2 eggs, whisked

Cooking oil

1 package organic broccoli florets

a few dashes TJ's Everyday Seasoning

1 pouch TJ's Rice Medley

1 teaspoon Sriracha and Roasted Garlic BBQ Sauce

TJ's Cilantro Dressing, to taste (optional)

Preheat oven to 350°F.

Rinse the chicken and pat dry.

Place cereal in a resealable plastic bag and roll into fine crumbs with a rolling pin. Pour crumbs into a bowl. Add the 21 Seasoning Salute and lemon zest, then add salt and pepper to taste.

Using tongs, dip each chicken breast into the egg and carefully dip into the cereal. Place the coated pieces on a baking sheet lined with parchment paper. Spray the top of chicken with cooking oil.

Bake 8–10 minutes or until the internal temperature reaches 165° F with a thermometer.

Once cooked, allow to cool about 2–3 minutes, then cut into slices. Portion out the chicken in containers to pack for lunch with fully cooked rice medley and some steamed broccoli according to package instructions. Portion out broccoli and top with Everyday Seasoning. Cook rice medley according to package instructions. Portion out and drizzle a little coconut oil overtop with some Himalayan pink salt and a little more lemon zest.

Drizzle Sriracha and Roasted Garlic BBQ Sauce over the chicken. If desired add a small container of dipping sauce, such as the Cilantro Dressing.

A bright and flavorful dish with a touch of sweetness from the kabocha squash and shrimp.

THAI RED CURRY with Roasted Kabocha Squash and Shrimp

1 cup kabocha squash, roasted, cut into 1-inch cubes or smaller pieces

8-10 raw frozen shrimp, tails on

2 teaspoons of sunflower seed oil

a dash of cayenne pepper

A dash or two of Himalayan pink salt, to taste

1-1½ cups TJ's Fire Roasted Peppers and Onions, thawed

2 teaspoons coconut sugar

½ bottle TJ's Thai Red Curry Sauce

2 sprigs of cilantro

1 pouch TJ's Sprouted Red Jasmine Rice, cook according to package instructions

a few lime wedges

10 TJ's Thai Lime and Chili Cashews, chopped

For instructions on roasting kabocha squash see the Breakfast Frittata recipe on page 18.

Thaw shrimp in cold water and then pat dry.

In a sauce pan or pot, heat oil over medium heat for 2 minutes. Add shrimp, cayenne pepper, and salt. Stir-fry approximately 3 minutes, stirring constantly. Once the shrimp turn pink and opaque, remove from the pan and set aside. Add peppers and onions and cook for 3 minutes. Add roasted squash, coconut sugar, and curry sauce, then return the shrimp to the pan. Reduce heat to simmer and cook 3–4 minutes, or until ingredients are heated through and shrimp are fully cooked and opaque.

Serve with rice and garnish with Thai Lime and Chili Cashews and cilantro. Squeeze lime directly onto bowl prior to eating.

Note: If you don't wish to cut and roast kabocha squash, use precut butternut squash! You can microwave them according to the package instructions, and then add them to the curry sauce.

Crunchy, sweet and not too spicy! The seasoned Curry Chicken Tenders from TJ's really dress up this salad. If you want more heat, simply add a few shakes of cayenne pepper or even more curry powder when mixing ingredients together.

CURRIED CHICKEN SALAD

1 package TJ's Curry Chicken Tenders

1 cup dried cranberries or TJ's Organic Thompson Seedless Raisins

¼ cup slivered almonds

½ cup dried apricots, sliced

1 granny smith apple, seeded, skin on, and diced

¼ cup plain, nonfat, Greek-Style yogurt

¼ cup organic mayonnaise

2 teaspoons apple cider vinegar

3 dashes of curry powder (optional)

½ package of romaine lettuce hearts

Preheat oven to 400°F.

Bake chicken tenders on parchment paper-lined baking sheet approximately 8 minutes or until they reach an internal temperature of 165°F. Once cooked, remove chicken from the oven and allow it to cool. Once it's cool, dice the chicken.

While the chicken is cooling, mix together the cranberries or raisins, almonds, apricots, apple, yogurt, mayonnaise, and vinegar in a large bowl. If desired, add curry powder. Add the cooled, diced chicken and stir just until it is blended in. Allow salad to chill. Serve in romaine lettuce hearts or other leafy greens.

Makes 3 servings

The wild mushrooms are wonderfully seasoned and have a little sauce with them! Use that to muddle with the barley on the plate.

GRILLED CHICKEN WITH
Barley and Mushroom Medley

3 TJ's skinless, boneless
  chicken breasts

olive oil

3 teaspoons TJ's Poultry Rub

canola cooking spray

1 package TJ's 10 Minute Barley

salt

pepper

½ package TJ's French Green
  Beans, thawed

3 dashes of lemon pepper

1 package TJ's Mushroom Medley

Pat the chicken dry, then drizzle a little olive oil on each side. Coat both sides of chicken with the Poultry Rub.

You can use an inside griddle to cook the chicken or bake it in the oven. For cooking on a griddle, spray the griddle with cooking spray and preheat it. Place the chicken on the heated griddle. Cook on each side for 6–8 minutes over medium heat. Cover while cooking to speed up cooking time. For oven baking, preheat the oven to 400°F. Bake chicken for 10 minutes, and then flip over and cook another 10 minutes. The chicken is done when the internal temperature reaches 165°F.

Follow package instructions for cooking barley. Add salt and pepper to taste.

Cook the green beans according to package instructions. Once cooked, toss them in a bowl with a little olive oil and lemon pepper.

Heat mushrooms according to package instructions.

For serving, place ½ cup barley on the plate and top with chicken, then add mushrooms and green beans on the side.

A high-fiber, go-to salad to enjoy any time of year, but nothing screams summer more than this! When you've got tons of tomatoes growing in the backyard and don't know what to do with them, just pull out this recipe. Tangy, creamy, crunchy—this salad has it all.

LENTIL SLAW
and Tomato Salad

½ package TJ's Steamed Lentils (in the refrigerated case)

1 small package of cherry or grape tomatoes, sliced in half

½ bag of shredded carrots

⅓ package of TJ's Cruciferous Crunch Collection

½ container TJ's Crumbled Goat Cheese

Combine all ingredients in a large bowl and set aside while you make the dressing.

½ small shallot, grated

1 teaspoon apple cider vinegar

1 teaspoon lemon juice

a pinch of lemon zest

1 tablespoon maple syrup or blue agave sweetener

1-2 dashes cayenne pepper

1 garlic clove smashed and minced

Himalayan pink salt

fresh cracked black pepper

For Shallot Vinaigrette Dressing

Whisk shallot, vinegar, lemon juice, lemon zest, maple syrup or agave, cayenne pepper and garlic together. Add salt and pepper to taste. Then, mix into bowl with salad ingredients.

Serve chilled.

Options: Experiment with dressings for this recipe. For example, Trader Joe's Balsamic Vinaigrette, or combine olive oil, garlic, and a splash of red wine with plenty of cracked pepper to give this salad an exquisite taste.

Makes 4 servings

No measurements needed for this quick and easy salad that's loaded with lean protein and fiber. I love the Organic Carrots of Many Colors! They taste the same to me as regular carrots, but sure are gorgeous when made into veggie "sketti" spirals. They make eating vegetables even more fun. Combined with the light, zesty Asian Vinaigrette, it's completely satisfying.

RAINBOW CARROTS
with Spicy Asian Vinaigrette

6 TJ's Organic Carrots of
Many Colors

1 cup fresh, raw edamame, seeded

3 teaspoons rice vinegar

2 teaspoons TJ's Toasted
Sesame Oil

TJ's Asian Style Spicy Peanut
Vinaigrette

a few dashes of cayenne pepper
(optional)

Use a Vegetti Spiral Vegetable Slicer or similar tool to make carrot "spaghetti." Toss the "spaghetti" in a bowl with the edamame. Add a few shakes of rice vinegar, toasted sesame seed oil, and vinaigrette. For extra heat, add a few shakes of cayenne pepper. Serve chilled.

Note: For more protein, add shrimp or cold white meat to the salad.

Makes 1 serving

You can make a less greasy, less fattening pizza at home in minutes using Trader Joe's Misto alla Griglia Marinated Grilled Eggplant and Zucchini (found in the freezer case). These veggies are marinated, grilled to perfection, and ready to use!

FLATBREAD PIZZA
with Grilled Eggplant and Zucchini

1 TJ's Whole Grain Flour
   Tortilla with Flaxseeds

1 teaspoon olive oil or
   cooking spray

¼ cup puttanesca sauce

3-4 pieces TJ's Misto alla Griglia
   Marinated Grilled Eggplant
   and Zucchini (freezer case),
   slightly thawed

crumbled goat cheese

2 teaspoons grated Parmesan
   cheese

2-3 TJ's Hot & Sweet Cherry
   Peppers, diced

5-6 thin slices of red onion

sprinkle of fresh red pepper flakes

2-3 leaves fresh basil, torn

Preheat oven to 400°F.

Place tortilla on a baking sheet. Coat the top with a little olive oil and bake until slightly golden and crunchy. Immediately remove and add sauce, then add the eggplant and zucchini, cheeses, peppers, onions, and pepper flakes. Bake 5–7 minutes, or until the cheese just begins to melt and the vegetables are warm.

Remove from the oven and add basil. Serve immediately while still crunchy and hot.

chapter

7

Date Night

Easy, sexy meals to
impress any date.

Makes 2 servings

The smoked paprika makes the perfect marriage between shrimp and butter. It is rounded out with a surprise lemony flavor. This is my favorite recipe in the book!

SMOKED PAPRIKA SHRIMP
with Zucchini "Spaghetti"

10 raw, shelled shrimp with tails on

grapeseed oil or olive oil

2 teaspoons clarified or regular butter

½ bag TJ's Fire Roasted Peppers and Onions, thawed

2 cloves of garlic, smashed and minced

a dash of cayenne pepper

teaspoon of fresh lemon juice

1-2 zucchinis

Himalayan pink salt, to taste

black pepper, to taste

Thaw shrimp in cold water, then pat dry.

In a saucepan, add the oil and shrimp. Cook over high heat until the shrimp are pink. Add in the butter and peppers and onions. Stir, then add in the garlic, cayenne pepper, and lemon juice. Cook approximately 5 minutes, until the shrimp are fully cooked and the vegetables are warmed through. Once done, remove from heat.

In a separate skillet, drizzle a little olive oil or butter. Place zucchini in a Vegetti vegetable spiral tool to form "spaghetti." Cook the zucchini spaghetti for 3–4 minutes over medium heat. Add salt and pepper to taste.

Place zucchini on plate and top with the shrimp mixture, along with some of the sauce. If desired, add a squirt of lemon before serving.

Makes 3-4 servings

This recipe works great on the grill, as the natural sugars from the cherrie get caramelized on the pork and produc a wonderful flavor!

PORK TENDERLOIN MEDALLIONS
with Rosemary Marinade

½ cup frozen, pitted dark
  cherries, thawed and blended
3 tablespoons olive oil
2 tablespoons honey
2 tablespoons plus 1 teaspoon
  apple cider vinegar
2 tablespoons fresh chopped
  rosemary
Himalayan pink salt
fresh cracked black pepper or
  rainbow cracked peppercorns
1 pork tenderloin, sliced into
  1-inch-thick pieces
12-inch wooden skewers, soaked
  in water for 30 minutes prior
  to grilling
canola cooking spray

Mix cherries, olive oil, honey, vinegar, and rosemary together in a bowl. Add salt and pepper to taste. Place the pork into the bowl and mix gently, ensuring the pork i coated with the marinade. Cover the bowl and refrigerate overnight.

Grilling the Medallions

Prior to grilling, remove the pork tenderloin medallions from the refrigerator and allow to sit at room temperature for 15 minutes. Put medallions widthwise on the soaked skewers.

Preheat gas grill on high with lid closed. If using a charcoal grill, prepare for direct heat cooking over hot charcoal.

Carefully coat the grill surface with cooking spray, spraying at an angle. Place the skewers directly over the heat. With the grill lid open, cook 3–4 minutes on one side and turn. After 3 minutes on the second side, check internal temperature. If internal temperature is 140–145°F, remove from heat immediately. Allow meat to rest for 5 minutes before serving.

Rosemary heirloom potatoes grilled in tinfoil with a little olive oil, salt, and pepper are the perfect side for these pork medallions.

Makes 2-3 servings

Lots of layers of flavor in these fun-to-cook parcels of fish! The parchment paper provides the perfect environment to seal in the flavors of garlic and tomatoes, creating wonderful, moist fish. Barramundi seems to come and go from the freezer case at Trader Joe's. Use mahi mahi if the barramundi is not available. Both are flaky, white, and sweet.

MEDITERRANEAN
Barramundi Parcels

1 package of frozen barramundi, thawed

olive oil

12-15 organic heirloom grape tomatoes, sliced in half

12-15 Kalamata pitted olives, sliced in half

5-7 slivers of red onion

5-8 fresh garlic cloves, cut into thin slices

1 wedge worth of fresh squeezed lemon juice per parcel

a few flakes of lemon zest

sprinkle of oregano in each parcel

sprinkle of dried or fresh thyme in each parcel

fresh cracked black pepper to taste

a dash of Himalayan pink salt

Preheat oven to 400°F.

Cut parchment paper into 8 x 12 inch rectangles. Place fish in the center of the paper, and then drizzle olive oil on top. Add a little of each of the ingredients, then fold up the parchment paper and fold the top over. Crimp the two ends. Place parcels in a 9 x 12 baking dish and bake 14–18 minutes. Peek into the parcels to check that the fish is done and the ingredients have broken down to create a sauce.

Remove from oven, and keep parcels closed to cook further while they rest. Allow to rest 3–5 minutes. Serve the closed paper parcel on a plate with a wedge of lemon.

Makes 4 servings

I don't eat too many things made with white potatoes, but every now and again I do enjoy gnocchi. Heirloom red spinach is loaded with antioxidants and iron. It comes and goes from Trader Joe's, but look for it in the summer. This recipe satisfies a pasta craving, but without too many calories from a heavy cheesy sauce.

GNOCCHI WITH ROASTED
Kabocha Squash

1 medium kabocha squash

canola cooking spray or TJ's Greek
  Kalamata Extra Virgin Olive Oil

1 17.6-ounce package of Gnocchi
  Italiani

4 tablespoons Earth Balance
  Buttery Spread or clarified
  butter

2 garlic cloves, smashed and minced

1 small pinch of nutmeg

8 large fresh sage leaves, diced
  and a few extra for garnish

¼ cup vegetable or chicken broth

a pinch of Himalayan pink salt

fresh cracked black pepper

1 bag TJ's Heirloom Spinach or
  regular baby spinach

¼ cup raw or roasted pumpkin
  seeds

Preheat oven to 400°F.

Carefully pierce the top of the squash with a large chef's knife and slice in half. Remove seeds and fibers, and then cut each half again, making 4 quarters. Coat with cooking spray and place on baking sheet. Bake approximately 20 minutes, until the squash is just turning tender. Remove from oven and allow squash to cool to the touch. Peel the skins off with a paring knife, then cut squash into 1-inch chunks.

Follow package instructions for cooking store-bought gnocchi. Some gnocchi comes fresh in the refrigerator case, while others may be found in the freezer case or grocery aisle in vacuum-packed packages.

In a large skillet, combine the spread or butter, garlic, nutmeg, diced sage, and vegetable broth. Cook over medium heat for 2-3 minutes. Add in the cooked gnocchi, salt, and pepper and stir to coat. Add the squash and spinach. The spinach will be heaping over the skillet at first, but will soon wilt down. Carefully stir to coat all ingredients.

Once spinach is wilted, toss in pumpkin seeds. Adjust seasoning to taste and serve immediately.

Makes 2 servings

The spicy cashews and mint with cilantro are a fun, fresh way to add zest to salmon.

SALMON PARCELS
with Cilantro Mint Pesto

1 cup fresh cilantro

1 cup fresh mint

2 teaspoons honey or agave nectar

a dash of salt

2 teaspoons TJ's Thai Lime and
   Chili Cashews

olive oil

---

3 cedar wraps with twine

1 package (usually 3 pieces)
   TJ's Wild Silverbrite Salmon,
   thawed

extra virgin olive oil

a pinch of Himalayan pink salt

fresh cracked black pepper

1 lemon, thinly sliced

Cilantro Mint Pesto

Blend cilantro, mint, honey or agave, salt and cashews in a food processor until smooth. Add a drizzle of olive oil to get the right consistency; it should be thick, but not too dry.

Salmon Parcels

Preheat oven to 400°F.

Soak grilling wrappers and the twine in water for 10 minutes. Place a cup of water on top of them to keep them submerged.

Once fish is thawed, remove fish from packaging and pat dry.

Line a baking sheet with parchment paper and place cedar wrappers on top. Place a piece of fish in the center of each cedar sheet. Top each one with a drizzle of olive oil, salt, and pepper, then add a lemon slice. Roll up each cedar wrap and tie with twine.

Bake for 6–9 minutes, or until the fish is firm and opaque. Once done, remove and place each parcel on a plate. Serve with cilantro mint pesto on top.

Note: If you grill these outside, place parcels directly onto grill rack and cook 3–4 minutes on each side. You'll get some nice grill marks and an extra punch of flavor!

Makes 3-4 servings

Pork tenderloin is a great lean protein that is often overlooked. It cooks fast, especially when cut into medallions, and it can take on so many flavors. In this case, I added Trader Joe's BBQ Rub and Seasoning with Coffee and Garlic. Yep, coffee! Don't worry, it won't keep you up all night; it has just a slight dusting of coffee with other spices to round it out.

PORK TENDERLOIN
with BBQ Coffee Rub

4–5 tablespoons TJ's BBQ Rub and Seasoning with Coffee and Garlic

3–4 tablespoons olive oil

1 pork tenderloin, sliced into 1-inch-thick medallions

12-inch wooden skewers, soaked in water for 30 minutes prior to grilling

Mix the rub and olive oil together in a bowl. Add pork and stir to make sure all pieces are coated. Cover and refrigerate for at least 1 hour.

Remove the pork tenderloin medallions from the refrigerator and allow to sit at room temperature for 15 minutes prior to grilling. Put medallions widthwise on the skewers.

Preheat gas grill on high with lid closed. If using a charcoal grill, prepare for direct heat cooking over hot charcoal.

Carefully coat the grill surface with cooking spray, spraying at an angle. Place the skewers directly over heat. With grill lid open, cook 3–4 minutes on one side and turn. After 3 minutes on the second side, check internal temperature. If internal temperature is 140–145°F, remove from heat immediately. Allow meat to rest for 5 minutes before serving.

These medallions are great served with grilled rosemary heirloom potatoes cooked in tinfoil with a little olive oil, salt, and pepper. To make the Tangy Cruciferous Slaw see page 66 in chapter 2.

Makes 2 servings

Spicy and rich! This dish is not quite as low in calories as some of the other recipes in this book, but it's tasty and baked, not fried. The cashews become more flavorful when cooked, and with the lime and chili flavor, you are in for an exquisite taste.

THAI LIME AND CHILI
Cashew-Crusted Chicken

1 cup plain, nonfat, Greek-style yogurt

2 skinless, boneless chicken breasts, cut in half

½ cup TJ's Thai Lime and Chili Cashews

Preheat oven to 425°F.

Place yogurt in a large bowl. Add chicken and coat lightly.

Grind cashews in a food processor, then place them on a plate.

Dip the chicken into the cashews to coat, and place on a parchment paper-lined baking sheet. Top with more of the ground cashews, tamping it into the chicken.

Cook 15–18 minutes or chicken reaches an internal temperature of 165°F.

Serve on top of Rainbow Carrots with Spicy Asian Vinaigrette. See page 68 for recipe.

Makes 3-4 servings

Who doesn't love a meal with an edible bowl? These butternut squash are a seasonal fall item. Trader Joe's has done all the hard work for you, and they come two to a package.

ROASTED BUTTERNUT
Squash Cups with Red Curry

1 package butternut squash cups

Precook the butternut squash cups according to package instructions.

Follow the recipe on page 130 to make the filling.

Fill each cup with filling and heat through in the oven for 8–10 minutes, then serve.

Makes 2 servings

The lemon and smoked paprika seem to be a nice marriage of flavors. The chicken will taste better if marinated overnight. Serve with steamed broccoli florets and TJ's Sprouted Red Jasmine Rice or Organic Brown Rice.

LEMONY SMOKED
Paprika Chicken

3 cloves of garlic, smashed and minced

½ teaspoon dried thyme

2 teaspoons ghee or regular butter

¼ teaspoon smoked paprika or more to taste

1 teaspoon extra virgin olive oil

1 teaspoon apple cider vinegar

2-3 fresh lemon wedges

Himalayan pink salt

pepper

cooking oil

2 skinless, boneless chicken breasts

Preheat oven to 400°F.

In a large bowl, combine the garlic, thyme, paprika, olive oil, vinegar, and the juice from the lemon wedges. Add a little salt and pepper. Add chicken and stir to coat all sides. Cover the bowl and refrigerate overnight.

Lightly coat a baking dish with cooking oil. Put the chicken and marinade into the dish. Add ghee over the chicken. Bake approximately 22 minutes, until core temperature of chicken reaches 165°F. Once cooked, allow chicken to rest a few minutes, then cut into slices. Plate with rice or quinoa and broccoli florets.

Follow package instructions for cooking the rice.

To steam broccoli, place florets in a sauce pan with ½ inch of water. Cook covered until broccoli is bright and slightly soft.

Makes 4 servings

Cauliflower crusts are popular on food blogs these days with so many people eating gluten-free. I wanted to offer a different twist, so I've used yogurt and some other Middle Eastern ingredients.

TUNISIAN PIZZA
with Cauliflower Crust

1 package TJ's Grilled Cauliflower (freezer case), thawed

½ cup grated Parmesan cheese

½ teaspoon TJ's 21 Seasoning Salute

2 eggs

½ teaspoon Himalayan pink salt

olive oil

For the Crust

Preheat oven to 450°F.

In a food processor, blend the cauliflower, cheese, and seasoning. Add the eggs and pulse just a little to blend.

Remove mixture and place on a baking sheet lined with parchment paper. Flatten and form a circle approximately 10 inches in diameter and ⅜ inch thick. Drizzle some olive oil over the top. Place on the middle rack of the preheated oven and cook until the edges begin to brown, 10–14 minutes.

To make the toppings, see page 210.

Continued from Breakfast Frittata recipe on page 18.

ROASTING MURASAKI SWEET POTATOES

½–¾ cup Murasaki sweet
potato

Preheat oven to 400°F.

I keep the skins on when I roast them. They have a wonderful purple color and add more fiber to your meal!

Scrub potatoes and rinse.
Cut into 1-inch cubes and place in a bowl. Toss with a little olive oil. Transfer cubes to a baking sheet lined with parchment paper. If desired, add salt and pepper. Cover lightly with tinfoil—do not seal. Bake for 12–15 minutes or until tender. Cook several potatoes at a time and store extra in the freezer for topping salads and mixing into recipes like the Farro Hash with Roasted Brussels Sprouts on page 48.

1 link All Natural Sweet
Apple Chicken Sausage

Cooking All Natural Chicken Apple Sausage

Dice sausage and place in a skillet. Cook over medium-high heat for 5 minutes or until crispy and brown on the edges. Feel free to cook the whole package of links and save the remaining pieces in the freezer for other recipes.

Note: a nonstick skillet works best for this recipe

Makes ½ cup

2 tablespoons lime juice

2 tablespoons lemon juice

½ teaspoon cumin

2 tablespoons apple cider
   vinegar

½ teaspoon shallot, finely minced

1 garlic clove, smashed and
   minced

1 teaspoon honey

½ teaspoon Himalayan pink salt

pepper

Continued from Salmon Salad with Corn and Chili Salsa with Lime Cumin Vinaigrette on page 46.

LIME CUMIN VINAIGRETTE

Whisk all ingredients together in a bowl. Dress the salad. Taste test. If desired, add more salt and pepper.

Optional: ½ teaspoon taco seasoning

Makes 6 servings

1 tablespoon apple cider vinegar

1 tablespoon honey

⅓ cup plain nonfat Greek-style
   yogurt

2 tablespoons organic mayonnaise

½ bag TJ's Cruciferous Crunch
   Collection

½ bag TJ's Shredded Carrots

Himalayan pink salt

black pepper

Continued from Carolina Gold BBQ Lettuce Wraps on page 136.

TANGY CRUCIFEROUS SLAW

Combine the vinegar, honey, yogurt, and mayonnaise in a large bowl. Add the veggies and toss to coat. Add salt and pepper to taste.

Options: TJ's Julienned Root Vegetables make a great side dish. You can find them in the freezer case.

Continued from Tunisian Pizza with Cauliflower Crust on page 206.

THE TOPPINGS

¼ cup plain, nonfat, Greek-style yogurt

4 tablespoons TJ's Hot & Sweet Mustard

2 teaspoons honey

2 cloves peeled garlic, minced

2 TJ's Preserved Lemon Slices, rinse, pat dry, then dice

3-4 tablespoons pistachios, roasted and salted

5-6 dried apricots, diced

sprinkle of fresh pomegranate seeds

2-3 teaspoons fresh mint, chopped

In a small bowl, mix the yogurt, mustard, honey, and garlic. Smear the yogurt mixture on top of the prepared crust. Add the prepared artichokes (instructions below) and lemon, then place back in the oven for 5 minutes. Remove from oven and top with pistachios, apricots, pomegranate seeds, and mint. Cut in wedges and serve immediately.

1-2 teaspoons olive oil

¾ package artichoke hearts (freezer case), thawed

1 teaspoon TJ's 21 Seasoning Salute

1 teaspoon butter

a few shakes of red pepper flakes

3-4 cranks of Himalayan pink salt

½ teaspoon fresh cracked black pepper

Artichokes

In a skillet over medium heat, add olive oil and artichokes. Cook 3 minutes. Add in seasoning and butter and cook another 3–4 minutes then set aside until you're ready to top the pizza.

INDEX